WRITER'S D

GUIDE TO
MAGAZINE
ARTICLE
WRITING

KERRIE FLANAGAN

**WRITER'S
DIGEST
BOOKS**

WRITER'S DIGEST BOOKS

An imprint of Penguin Random House LLC
penguinrandomhouse.com

ISBN 978-1-4403-5124-2

Printed in the United States of America

Edited by Melissa Wuske and Amy Jones
Designed by Liz Harasymczuk and Alexis Estoye

DEDICATION

To writers, past, present, and future, whose inquisitive nature fills the pages of magazines with information, inspiration, and fascinating curiosities.

ACKNOWLEDGMENTS

This book is a dream come true for me and one that would not have been accomplished without the tremendous support system I have. Since the beginning of my writing journey two decades ago my husband, Rich, has been there for me. Through the ups and downs, lefts, rights, and all the other directions writing can take a person, he stuck by me. Thank you, Dear!

Every writer needs a community, a tribe, people who understand and are there to push you through the tough times and share the champagne when it's time to celebrate the successes. I am incredibly fortunate to have this. To my Wednesday Group (past and present), this book would have never happened without you. Twenty years ago you accepted me into your writing family and mentored me, guided me, and believed in me. Ellen, LeAnn, Carol, Linda, Jenny, Liz, Helen, Carol S., Sally, and Margaret, I am grateful for your support and friendship over the years.

To the Enders: Chuck, Jenny, Kelly, and Dean, your insight and critique made this book stronger and your friendship and support got me through those times I felt discouraged. Chuck, thanks for helping me create and stick to a writing schedule to finish this manuscript and for holding me accountable (even though at times I kicked and screamed and whined about it).

A big thank-you to April Moore and the Northern Colorado Writers. It is great to be part of such a supportive and encouraging organization.

I am indebted to Phil Sexton and Rachel Randall who believed in this project and gave it the initial green light. Thank you, Melissa, for your keen editing eye and helping to iron out the final details. I appreciate all the writers, editors, and professionals who took the time to answer my questions and were willing to share their insight with the readers of this book.

And finally, a big, big thanks to my parents. Growing up, they allowed me the freedom to explore a variety of interests from soccer to drawing to music. They were always there to support and encourage me, building my confidence and instilling in me this idea that no dream was too big, and this book proves they were right. Thanks, Mom and Dad!

ABOUT THE AUTHOR

Kerrie Flanagan is an author, writing consultant, publisher, and accomplished freelance writer with nearly two decades of experience. Her writing has appeared on the pages of *Writer's Digest*, *Chicago Tribune*, *FamilyFun*, *Alaska* magazine, *Writer's Market*, six *Chicken Soup for the Soul* books, and *Better Homes and Gardens* among many others.

She is the author of eight books, all published under her label, Hot Chocolate Press (hotchocolatepress.com). In addition to her own writing, she is passionate about helping other writers. She founded Northern Colorado Writers and was the director of the organization for ten years. Now she does individual writing consultations and hosts retreats.

When Kerrie is not writing articles, presenting at conferences, or working with other writers, you can find her fly-fishing on a river, enjoying wine with friends, camping in the beautiful Colorado mountains with her family, traveling or hanging out with her husband and adult children.

If you are interested in contacting Kerrie about a consultation, have a question relating to this book, or you are interested in having her speak at a writing event, you can reach her at kerrie.flanagan @gmail.com. To find out where she is presenting next or current projects she is working on, visit KerrieFlanagan.com.

TABLE OF CONTENTS

FOREWORD

In 2003, I wasn't an online magazine editor just yet. I'd whittled my day job in advertising down to two days a week and was carving my path into full-time freelancing. My niche was in the action sports industry. It was by accident, really. My husband was the marketing director for a skateboard shoe company, and I tagged along to skateboarding competitions and trade shows. Being in the scene gave me ideas and introductions. I crafted pieces that were published in magazines, like *Transworld Skateboarding, Thrasher*, and *Vice Magazine*, as well as trade publications, like *Footwear News*. I wrote company newsletters and ad copy. I subcontracted photographers and videographers to create irresistible content packages and marketing materials. And within the first year of freelancing, I made more than $75,000, which was more money than I'd ever made in a single year.

At the same time, I wrote fiction. I wanted to be the next Chuck Palahniuk, writing dark and twisty tales *in media res* with characters who'd been marginalized by society and reacted with self-destructive aggressiveness. In fact, my style was so similar to his that several writers in an online writer's forum wondered if I was him! I obviously hadn't cultivated my own voice yet, but I managed to get several short stories published in literary journals. I was thrilled. I wanted to immerse myself in the literary world of critique groups, contests, conferences, and workshops. I wanted to meet publishing industry professionals.

In September 2006, my business partner and I launched WOW! Women On Writing—an online magazine for writers, authors, editors, agents, publishers, and readers—because there was nothing like it at the time. Our mission was to give women writers a platform to share their professional knowledge with one another. Since then, WOW has evolved into a gender fluid space, grown exponentially and won awards, including the *Writer's Digest* 101 Best Sites for Writers award for more than eight years. As executive editor, I've personally worked with hundreds of talented writers. One of the most creative and professional freelancers I've had the pleasure of working with is the author of this book, Kerrie Flanagan.

In 2009, Kerrie sent a letter of introduction that caught my attention. She talked about her passion for helping writers, her 100+ clips, and her experience starting the Northern Colorado Writers (NCW) organization. She wrote about an NCW conference, where she mingled with authors and agents and pitched article ideas for our various departments. Honestly, what impressed me about her letter was our shared vision of helping writers and her impressive knowledge of the industry, plus the names she mentioned didn't hurt. I wanted to get to know those agents, and I knew our readers did, too. That sparked an idea. I wrote her back immediately and asked her to write the article, "How to Pitch an Agent at a Writers' Conference" for our "Agents & Authors" December '09 issue. I suggested she use tips from her NCW conference workshop and agent interviews in the article. She delivered exactly what I envisioned, and our relationship was sealed.

When an editor finds a freelancer who delivers polished articles on time and is a pleasure to work with, it's magical. The formalities disappear, and it's just a matter of putting your heads together and creating great content. Kerrie's strength is coming up with creative ideas that I never would have. Her vision inspires mine. Plus, she's a phenomenal writer, and her writing style is friendly and knowledgeable, as you'll soon see in this book.

If you are a writer just starting out or have some clips, but want to land better assignments, this book is gold. As someone who's worked on both sides of the desk, I can tell you that Kerrie's advice will save you years of learning the hard way.

Take special note of the chapter on querying since this will be your very first impression with editors. I hate to sound like a grumpy gatekeeper, but in recent years I've seen a lack of query etiquette. Out of every hundred query letters I read, maybe five are professional with ideas that target our e-zine's content and audience. The rest are for subjects like yoga mats and feminism, or state: "I want to write for you. How do I get paid?" Flinging your work like wet pasta out into the publication world and hoping it sticks doesn't work.

If you follow the steps in this book, you will be successful. I've never read a book this in-depth on the subject of writing articles for magazines. Kerrie shows you how to study a magazine (in an ingenious way I haven't heard of before) and walks you through each step, providing worksheets to help you track a publication's needs. She chats with amazing writers, like Andrew McCarthy who shares a kernel that will change the way you think about beginning an article. The editor round-ups are priceless. Editors from publications, like *The Costco Connection* and *Condé Nast Traveler*, share their best tips. It feels like you're sitting across from them having coffee.

And that's not all. Kerrie provides you with the tools to succeed as a freelancer, including practical tips on goal setting, productivity, and awakening your creative muse. There's also a chapter on writing and selling personal essays that reads like a mini-book. The chapter on writing for online markets highlights the differences between print and online; and finally, there is a fascinating chapter on using article writing to build a platform. If you are a fiction writer, you will learn how to pull topics from your novel to craft articles that will help you find readers. And that's what we all ultimately want, right? To find readers. To build our tribe. To share our ideas with the world.

There's an inspirational quote from *Harry Potter* author J.K. Rowling: "Anything's possible if you've got enough nerve."

Writing and submitting certainly takes nerve, and the possibilities are endless, but courage is not enough. It also takes know-how. That's what this book can provide. Mix in a dash of determination and a pinch of persistence, and you've got a winning recipe for freelancing success.

Follow the advice in this book and get your words published.

Write on!

—Angela Mackintosh
Editor-in-Chief, WOW! Women On Writing
www.wow-womenonwriting.com

INTRODUCTION

I never wanted to be a writer. I am not one of those people who knew from childhood that this was the profession for me. Don't get me wrong; I liked writing and English classes throughout school. I even loved diagramming sentences, but I never fantasized about being the next C.S. Lewis or Laura Ingalls Wilder (two of my favorite authors growing up).

From as early as I can remember, I dreamed of being a teacher. I played school with my friends, and I loved writing on chalkboards. Teaching ran through my blood. My mom was a teacher in addition to my uncle, his wife, and my aunt. They all taught in public schools. I was destined to follow in my family's footsteps and eventually achieved this dream.

The writing door cracked open while I was student teaching a class of second graders. One of my tasks included teaching them how to use a comma in a list. Eight-year-olds don't really care about punctuation, so I wanted to find a creative way to get the point across to them. I wrote a story, made some simple cutout illustrations to go with it, and brought it to class.

Cornelius Comma Saves the Day was a big hit with the kids and my supervising teacher. I found it helpful in teaching the lesson and thought other educators would as well. I researched how to get it published. I read everything I could on the subject, found suitable publishers in the educational market and sent out queries. Mainstream e-mail and Internet didn't exist at that time, so I sent everything out snail mail and waited for responses. The *no thank yous* trickled in, and I sent out more queries until I finally exhausted the educational book market.

Not one to give up, I decided to self-publish *Cornelius*. There was no print-on-demand, Google, or Facebook. Determined to get the book into the hands of teachers, I found an illustrator and a printer.

Around this same time, I joined a critique group. Because the writing world was so new to me, I figured I needed all the help and support I could get. The group met every Wednesday from seven to ten in the evening and included writers of different genres: children's, romance, historical fiction, personal essays, and magazines.

The comma book sold a couple thousand copies, and the illustrator and I eventually moved on to other projects. I continued attending the writers' group and became intrigued by the idea of writing for magazines. One woman in the group frequently brought in articles for us to critique. I loved the time frame of it all: send out a query, get the assignment, write the article, and see it in print. The entire process from start to finish averaged four to six months, much faster than the book world. Plus it easily fit into my life, which now included a full-time teaching job, a husband, and three kids.

I wanted to learn more. I took a few months to better understand how writing and selling magazine articles worked. I read books and studied the best way to write for magazines, attended classes, a conference, read magazines, and learned more about the process. When I felt ready, I invested in a copy of *Writer's Market*, scoured the consumer and trade magazine section, and made a list of potential publications to query.

Armed with an idea and my newfound knowledge, I went to my writers' group and told them I had something ready to send out. They asked me to share my plan.

"I have a craft idea for a handprint wreath that I want to send to *Better Homes and Gardens*," I told them. "It's perfect for their family section toward the back of the magazine."

They all shook their heads and gave me a bless-your-new-little-writing-heart look.

"You can't send something to *Better Homes and Gardens*," said one group member.

"Why not?" I asked.

"Because," said another, "that's one of the top magazines. You don't start with one like that. Try a regional magazine or something smaller."

"But I did my research, and it's a perfect fit," I said. "I read back issues, and they have published other craft ideas similar to this."

"Still," said another member, "you don't have much of a chance with one like this."

"I want to try," I said.

And try I did. I found the name of the editor for that department and directed the cover letter to him. I printed it off, included it with the idea, and put it in the mail. Then I waited. And waited.

A couple of weeks later, I received a call from the editor telling me he wanted to publish my craft idea. I could hardly contain my excitement while he gave me all the details. As soon as I hung up, I danced around the house. I was going to be published in *Better Homes and Gardens*! When I shared this with my writers' group, they were surprised and thrilled for me. I trusted my research, didn't overthink it when it was time to send my work (I seldom do), and the timing happened to work out perfectly.

The piece that ended up in *Better Homes and Gardens* wasn't Pulitzer-quality writing. It consisted of about 150 words. But it allowed me to say I was published in a prestigious national magazine. It opened up a new world to me. It showed me that I could submit ideas and queries to any publication and have a good chance of getting a *yes* if I did my research, studied the magazines, and sent my ideas only to those that were a good fit. I never published another craft idea or article in *Better Homes and Gardens*, but it gave me the confidence to write for other magazines and a great clip to include in future queries. Not long after, I received an assignment to write a feature about Colorado wineries for a regional publication, *Colorado Homes & Lifestyles*.

For two years following that first article, I published twelve more articles in a variety of magazines including *Family Motor Coaching*, a children's magazine called *Crinkles*, a few more in *Colorado Homes & Lifestyles*, *Woman's World*, and even the *Chicago Tribune*. Trying to fit in writing with my life at home and work became a challenge. I realized I couldn't give the necessary attention to all of these areas. So after eight years as an elementary school teacher, I resigned to be more available to my family and to pursue writing part-time. Being able to take my kids to school and be there for them after school was important to me. It gave me time during the day to continue to write. I even branched out into PR writing when I took a part-time job with our local visitors' bureau; it was a job I could do while the kids were in school.

Over the past two decades, I have written for national, regional, local, and niche trade magazines, and blogs, in addition to PR writing. I wouldn't change anything about my writing journey because I learned so much along the way, especially as the industry evolved. Certain aspects are different now: I rarely send queries through the mail anymore, communication is done through e-mail, there are now online opportunities, and I can do a lot of my research on the Internet. Regardless of the changes, the core method remains the same.

You can't jump into something new and become an expert right away. But the only way to improve is to get in there and go for it. Magazine writing is no different. Once you understand how the process works, your odds for acceptance increase. You have nothing to lose by giving it a try.

This book provides you the necessary information for heading down the path of magazine writing, even in today's ever-changing market. The examples throughout will help you better understand the various kinds of articles while including valuable information about the craft and how to succeed.

When you stay open to new ideas and directions, you may end up places you never expected. If you had asked me twenty years ago what I would be doing with my life, I would have said teaching. But now I can't imagine my life without writing. I love what I do, and if I can write for magazines, you can do the same.

Happy Writing!

Kerrie

CHAPTER ONE

WHY WRITE FOR MAGAZINES?

Why write for magazines? I guess the bigger question is, why not? There are thousands of print and digital magazines, and they all have one thing in common. They need writers. And the fact that these publications continue to put out new issues monthly, quarterly, and some weekly, means they need a continuous stream of quality content from good writers.

In this age of digital media, there is a misconception that magazines, like newspapers, are dying a slow death, especially with young readers. A recent report from The Association of Magazine Media dispels this myth and illustrates the growth and vibrancy of this market. Currently there are more than seven thousand print magazines in the United States. Ninety-one percent of U.S. adults read print magazines with the biggest readership in the thirty-five and under crowd. The net audience for both print and digital editions has grown to more than 215 million and continues to grow.

EDITORS NEED WRITERS

This is good news! With the popularity of magazines, more content is going to be needed from writers who understand the industry. Editors look for writers who know how to write an effective query, who take the time to research their publication, who can expand on a good idea, who are capable of writing a great piece, and who respect word count and deadlines. Editors seek writers who will make their jobs easier by being professional and easy to work with.

Of the more than seven thousand print magazines in the United States, many are niche and trade publications you may not have heard of before. These magazines focus on a narrowly defined topic or specialty. You won't find these at Barnes & Noble or at your local newsstand. But there are magazines on every topic you can imagine. *The Concrete Producer, Bee Culture, The American Window Cleaner Magazine, Balloons and Parties Magazine, Military Vehicles Magazine, Sky & Telescope,* and *Sand Sports Magazine* are just a few of these unique publications. Unlike the well-known magazines you see in the grocery store, like *Family Circle* or *Prevention*, these smaller publications aren't inundated with freelance writers knocking down the door. This makes them more open to working with new writers, especially ones who take the time to understand their readership and their magazine. If you have a hobby or special interest, chances are there are magazines published on the topic, and you're ideally suited to write for them.

"Niches are great because they're much less competitive than larger markets," says Megan Hill, freelance writer from Seattle. "You can more easily differentiate yourself among the competition and be a big fish in a small pond."

QUICK TURNAROUND

If you are someone who likes short-term projects and quick turnarounds, then you will enjoy this line of work. Unlike publishing a book, which can take years, writing for magazines is a shorter process from start to finish. From writing the initial query to seeing your article in print can take as little as a few months. With digital magazines, this can be even shorter. If you like to get things done and move on to the next project, this is appealing. Plus you don't have to worry about investing a lot of time in an idea that doesn't pan out.

Magazines have different lead times. This refers to how far in advance they are working on an issue. Some work four to six months out and for others it may be a month. For publications with longer lead times, it's possible you will have two to three months to work on the piece before turning it in. For those with a shorter lead time, you may be given a couple of weeks to turn around the article. Regardless of the lead time, the process from query to publication is still relatively short.

NEW EXPERIENCES AND NEW PEOPLE

Writing for magazines can open up a new world for you. Over the years I have had the privilege of interviewing some wonderful people who have inspired and encouraged me, and some have even become my friends. I have met celebrities, business owners, artists, authors, and everyday people with extraordinary stories. With each one I feel more connected to those around me and my worldview expands.

There's advice floating around that says, *write what you know*, but that should be expanded to *write what you want to know*. In my local paper, years ago, was an article about Colorado wineries. After reading it, I wanted to know more about this topic. After all, I enjoyed a good glass of wine after work or with dinner. Having wineries nearby meant I could learn more without having to travel far. I researched the industry, wrote a query and received an assignment. I learned so much doing the article. Did you know that Colorado vineyards are the highest in terms of altitude in the northern hemisphere? And that the climate on the western slopes of Colorado near Grand Junction is ideal for grape growing? Winery owners took me on private tours, and sampling a Viognier right out of the barrel is an experience I'll never forget.

Through my articles I have learned about the Alaska Marine Highway, how to write for the children's app market, interesting facts about the Tongass National Forest, RV safety, and so much more. Getting paid to write the articles is great, but it goes beyond the money. I love the experiences afforded to me because of my magazine writing. With each new assignment comes the chance to expand my knowledge and learn more about the world and the people who live here.

YOU DON'T NEED A JOURNALISM DEGREE

The good news is that to venture into this world of magazine writing, you don't need a degree in journalism. I have a bachelor's degree in social science along with a teaching certificate. Editors have never asked about my degree. They look for well-written pieces that will be of interest to their readers.

You don't need an advanced or specialized degree, or even a college diploma, but you do need solid writing skills and a curiosity about the world around you. Your degree, if you have one, along with your unique life experiences, provides you with topics and article ideas where you might be considered an expert. Maybe you have been fly-fishing since you were a kid. Or you are a video game fanatic. Or you have six children (who are polite and well-behaved). These are all areas that don't require a degree, and readers of certain magazines would be interested to learn more from you.

Using your life experiences, your knowledge, and exploring areas you want to know more about gives you unique ideas and expertise that editors will welcome.

FOR THE LOVE OF RESEARCH

There is something exciting about gathering all the necessary information for an article. For me it's the thrill of the hunt, which can involve research on the computer, talking with experts, traveling to a destination, seeking facts, or collecting materials.

Years ago, we went on a trip to Alaska. While there, I picked up brochures everywhere we went, talked with the locals, jotted down notes, took photos, and experienced as much as I could. When I returned home I had a good collection of material and information. I then took one month and focused all my energy and queries on Alaska. I organized my notes, looked through the brochures and figured out potential story angles. I ended up with a feature assignment about traveling the Alaska Marine Highway that was published in a trade magazine, *Family Motor Coaching*. And just recently (ten years after this trip) I received an assignment with *Alaska* magazine to write about the Tongass National Forest, based on an idea that surfaced during that vacation. After initially sending out queries for this idea following the trip and getting "no thank yous," I put the query away. Every now and then I would think about it and send it out again. But nothing ever surfaced. Then at a writing conference I was talking with the editor of *Alaska* magazine. I shared with her that I had always wanted to write an article about the Tongass rainforest since visiting there. We talked and I told her I had queried the idea but never had found anyone interested in it. She said it could be a good fit for a specific department in her magazine if I changed the slant. We talked through it and by the end of the conversation, I had the assignment.

Researching and gathering information is what keeps writing for magazines interesting. It becomes a big puzzle with many moving parts, and then the fun comes when it's time to put all those pieces together into one article readers will enjoy.

I was working on an article for a writing magazine on the topic "Does social media really work?" My goal was to explore whether it was necessary for authors to participate on Twitter, Facebook, Instagram, and other platforms to be successful. I knew this was a huge topic that would take some digging and end up with a lot of moving parts. One question (along with a few others) I put out to writers, agents, and editors was "Have you seen a difference in sales for your authors (or yourself, if it went to an author) who are more active on social media? Please explain." The overwhelming response to that specific question was, "no," which was what I suspected.

Subsequently the big question in my head was why do people continue to do social media? In the follow-up, "Please explain," I received other helpful information that addressed my new question. Turns out, it was more about connecting with readers (which could happen on social media, but not always) and good writing. Once I got all my answers, I had to look them over carefully, determine the commonalities and differences, and put my conclusions into an interesting article for the reader.

MONEY

Magazine writing is great, but it is work. There is nothing wrong with getting paid for your time and effort. Often writers have this idea that because it is a creative venture, they shouldn't expect to get paid. Magazines are a business and because of that you deserve compensation. This can range from ten dollars for an article up to one thousand dollars or more. You probably aren't going to get a top rate straight out of the chute, but it is something to work toward. Getting paid to have your work in the hands of readers is a definite perk. Plus this money can be a good way to supplement your income alongside a full-time job.

FLEXIBLE HOURS

The beauty of magazine writing is that you decide how much time you are putting into it. You choose how many assignments you want. Maybe you want to start with one a month or maybe you want to jump all the way in and get as many as you can. When I first started,

I was a full-time teacher, wife, and mother of three; writing was something I did on the side. I worked on one article at a time. That year I had seven assignments, which was perfect. It allowed me to devote time and energy to my family and my career, while having this small job just for me.

If you are interested in being a full-time freelance writer, it will take months to gear up to this by sending out dozens of queries and making connections with editors. Debbie Hanson, a freelance writer from Florida, says, "It's important to have a high degree of patience when starting out. Don't expect a freelance writing career to take off overnight. It takes time to build credibility and editorial contacts."

Whether you write for magazines part-time or full-time, you control your schedule and how much work you accept. The flip side is the work can be inconsistent, and you have to be prepared for that as well.

WORKING FROM HOME (OR ON THE ROAD)

Magazine writing is a freelance endeavor that is done from home. This provides you many freedoms and options you wouldn't have otherwise. Depending on how far your work space is from your bedroom, there isn't a long commute each morning. If you work in your pajamas, no one cares, plus it saves money on work clothes. You can structure your work space and workday in whatever way suits your personality, strengths, and your family or household commitments.

When you are tired of looking at the same four walls, you can take your computer on the road to a local coffee shop or library (though you will want to change out of your pajamas). If you want to travel, then by all means, pack up your laptop and go see the world. It will give you great material and ideas to work with, and you can still write and submit queries.

Magazine writing is an area of the publishing world that is open to all writers. More than seven thousand print magazines and all digital publications need well-written content, and editors look for professional, competent writers to provide it. Why write for magazines? Because you can. With the right knowledge (found in this book) and preparation, seeing your byline on the pages of a magazine, either print or digital, is definitely possible.

WHY I LOVE WRITING FOR MAGAZINES

INSIGHT FROM FREELANCE WRITERS

JORDAN ROSENFELD: I love generating new ideas and the "high" of a pitch that is accepted. I love interviewing people and consolidating data into a digestible outcome. I love the freedom and flexibility to set my own schedule.

DANIELLE BRAFF: I love that I can write about anything I want. For example, whenever I have a problem with my kids, I write an article about it so that I can spend time speaking with all the experts. I just finished writing an article for the *Chicago Tribune* about sibling rivalry because my children can't stop arguing. I got to interview a bunch of different child psychologists and other experts to get lots of different opinions on how to get this to stop.

MEGAN HILL: I like doing something different every day, and there's constantly an element of excitement that keeps me on my toes. I've got a great rotating stable of consistent projects that I love, and random new possibilities pop into my in-box every week. It's thrilling! I also love being my own boss and dictating how I spend my time. I don't ever feel my time is wasted. If I finish my work early, I can leave my office and go do something fun or relaxing, rather than feeling forced by office peer pressure to "look busy" for eight hours a day, five days a week.

TOM KEER: I think of print books, print magazines, digital magazines, blogs, and social media (among others) as pearls that become a necklace with a piece of thread. The thread that turns those individual pearls into a necklace is the creative process, and that is what I love about writing. I love moving along the path that takes me from a rough idea to a completed manuscript.

ROXANNE HAWN: The flexibility to structure my days and my life. I like not having to wear professional clothes, especially tights or hose.

MICKEY GOODMAN: Everything! I loved interviewing the dignitaries and famous visitors to campus like Malcolm X, The Kingston Trio, the prime minister of Indonesia—and seeing my byline in print. It was especially exciting when the AP and UPI (this was in the early sixties) picked up my stories for wider distribution. The most widely printed were a retrospect of Malcolm X after his murder and a series of articles I wrote about the studies underway at UNC Medical Center, including one of the first on autism.

STACEY MCKENNA: I adore the schedule—both setting my own hours and days. But I also appreciate the intellectual freedom. Freelancing lets me pursue the reaches of my curiosity. I love that each story opens new trails to be explored.

DEBBIE HANSON: Being able to share my experiences and knowledge through the written word.

AMANDA CASTLEMAN: I love the freedom to organize my day, pursue stories I'm passionate about, and travel the world.

Article Example: FOB (Front of the Book)

BASIC PROCESS OF MAGAZINE WRITING, A QUICK OVERVIEW

The number of magazines is on the rise, giving writers more opportunities for publication. It is helpful to understand the basic process of publishing an article before exploring this option. We'll explore this in depth in the chapters ahead, but here is a quick overview of the process.

IDEA: There are really no new ideas, but there are plenty of new ways to slant them. It is important to find a unique angle that makes your article stand out and one that hasn't been covered by the magazine recently.

QUERY: This is a one-page sales pitch to the editor of a magazine. It gives an initial hook, an overview of the idea, the basic direction of the article, and what qualifies you to write it.

ASSIGNMENT: If an editor likes your idea, she will offer you a contract that spells out what she wants in regard to word count, deadline, and payment. Once the contract is signed, you can move on to the article.

WRITE ARTICLE: Now it's time to put together all the information you collected. Stay within your assigned word count and send the article to the editor before the deadline.

REVISIONS: There may be sections of your article the editor wants you to rework. It's all part of the process and isn't a reflection on your skills as a writer. Work as quickly as possible to get the revisions done and back to the editor.

SEE IN PRINT OR ONLINE: About two to six months after you turn in the article and the revisions are complete, you will see it in the magazine. For print you typically receive a free contributor copy.

PAYMENT: This occurs in one of two ways. Payment on acceptance means you receive your check soon after the article is sent and the editor accepts it. Payment on publication means you receive your money about thirty days after it is printed and released.

REPEAT: To build a relationship with this editor, research another idea and send her a new query soon after your article is revised and accepted.

CHAPTER TWO

WHAT'S THE BIG IDEA?

Ideas are at the core of everything you do as a writer, and they're what will keep you busy and get you published. Gathering them is not difficult, but it takes some direction and maybe even a shift in your thinking to see the wealth of ideas around you. You can find ideas at the grocery store, your kid's school, on the radio, and everywhere you go. As your awareness heightens, ask yourself questions like *why, how, where,* and *who*. Look at situations and people with a deeper curiosity and story ideas will emerge. Have a notebook, the recorder on your phone, or your camera handy to save your findings.

Here are a few great ways to begin your quest.

LIFE

Everyday life provides an abundance of ideas: From a grocery store to a movie theater to a concert in the park, ideas are all around you. Approach your day and situations with a sense of wonder; play around with different story slants and angles. Take the perspective of different types of magazines: travel, women's, parenting, business, gardening, craft. What insights can you glean? What would interest different kinds of readers? What unique perspective can you offer?

If you want to write travel articles, start close to home. What activities are in your area? Is there outdoor recreation? Museums?

Music? What is the history of your city or town? When was it formed? If you are thinking about parenting articles, find the activities and events geared toward children and families, and learn more about those. For business magazines find the main industries in your area. How big are the companies? What are their missions? How do they give back to the community? Are there interesting stories about how they each began?

Focus on your hobbies and extracurricular activities. Are you a watercolor artist? Do you enjoy woodworking? Do you spend time building model cars or creating quilts? Do you enjoy digging into your family tree? There are magazines devoted to all these topics, and they appreciate article ideas from writers who understand and enjoy these interests.

Day-to-day life provides a wealth of article ideas. There are common issues and challenges many face: child care, transportation, meal prep, budgeting, relationships, staying healthy, parenting. The list could go on. Think about these and what you can write to provide insight, solutions, or perspective to readers.

Birthdays are a big deal at our house, and this was especially true when our kids were young. We hosted a party for them and their friends each year. Costs became an issue the older they became. When our daughter was eight years old and our son was ten, my husband came up with a solution. Give them a birthday budget of fifty dollars to spend however they want on their parties. This turned out to be a great answer to our dilemma and ended up as an article for *FamilyFun* magazine.

Here is a chart to get you thinking about the different aspects of your life that might spark article ideas. Later in the chapter we will discuss how to use an idea map to narrow down broad topics into manageable, salable ideas.

LIST 4 OF YOUR FAVOR-ITE HOBBIES				
ORGANIZATIONS YOU ARE INVOLVED IN (CHURCH, SCHOOL PROFESSIONAL ORGANIZATIONS, CIVIC GROUPS ...)				
4 PLACES YOU HAVE TRAVELED				
4 PLACES YOU WANT TO TRAVEL				
OCCUPATION YOU CURRENTLY HAVE AND 3 YOU HAVE HAD				
SPORTS YOU CURRENTLY PLAY OR HAVE PLAYED				
INSTRUMENTS YOU PLAY OR HAVE PLAYED				
SKILLS YOU HAVE (WELD-ING, DANCING, COOK-ING ...)				
CAUSES YOU ARE PASSIONATE ABOUT				
ANIMALS YOU HAVE AND/OR FIND FASCINAT-ING				
ACTIVITIES YOU DO FOR FUN				
4 CHALLENGES YOU CONTINUALLY STRUG-GLE WITH (TIME MAN-AGEMENT, ORGANIZA-TION, DIET ...)				
FAVORITE HOLIDAYS AND/OR EVENTS				

NEWSPAPERS

Daily news, whether it's print or online, can provide a wealth of article ideas. Skim the headlines of your local paper to find interesting topics or subjects. Many times you will find stories of people in your community who have overcome incredible challenges or who have achieved great success. These are potential profiles in national magazines or trade publications that focus on specific aspects of their stories. Look at events in your area. My local paper recently highlighted information about an upcoming corgi parade. This sparked a few ideas: history of corgis, ten corgis and their famous owners, tips on caring for your corgi. ... From this one headline, many topics surfaced.

Read through national and local headlines to see the topics being covered. Have there been any breakthroughs in medicine? What topics are trending in business, education, travel, or politics? Are there interesting people being profiled? The newspaper has clearly covered the topic mentioned in the headline, but what other angles come to mind based on those headlines?

Keep in mind that while the turnaround for magazines is quick, newspapers are quicker. Although topics are easy to transfer between the two, you'll want to be sure your angle won't be old news by the time a magazine comes out. That's a sure way to have your query rejected.

Here are three headlines and the ideas that come to mind:

1. "On the Trail of Famous Women" (the article covered National Park Service sites that highlighted various women in history)

   - Marjory Stoneman and her book *The Everglades: River of Grass*
   - Roundup highlighting ten of the sites

2. "Homeowners on the Move Are Choosing More Affordable States"

   - How to find affordable housing in your area
   - Top ten states with the most affordable housing
   - Five things to look for in a moving company
   - Ten ways to ease the stress of moving for your children

3. "Ten Ways to Improve Your Relationships Now"

- • Tips to improve your relationship with your siblings
- • Five things you are doing to sabotage your relationships
- • Best advice to give to your teens before they start dating
- • Three ways to heal a wounded relationship

A few years back, an article appeared in my local paper about a group of parents suing a big media and television company. They claimed that putting cartoon characters' images on junk food packaging contributed to childhood obesity. As a mother of three, I read this and became angry that these parents were passing on the blame for their children's poor eating habits and obesity. They were teaching their children that they did not have to accept responsibility for their choices. This rolled around in my mind for a couple of days, and I couldn't let it go. I wrote an essay about this lawsuit and how I felt about it. Then I found an online magazine, *Imperfect Parent*, that accepts pieces like this. They liked it, published it, and I received payment for it.

MAGAZINES

Read through magazines to explore the current or hot topics being covered. Maybe you find a cover line about the five best national parks in the United States to visit in the fall. This article has been done, but are there other ideas using this basic concept? What about picking one of the parks highlighted in the article and doing a longer piece about it for another magazine? Research the history, talk with a ranger to get insider information about the park, learn about the wildlife, explore the recreational opportunities there, read about the vegetation, or find out about new attractions or environmental initiatives at the park.

How about creating a more local angle by covering the five best state parks in your state? Change the season and go with the five best national parks to visit in the winter. Take another approach with the five best national parks to view wildlife. There are many possibilities based on the one title found on the cover.

NONFICTION BOOKS

Visit the nonfiction section of your local bookstore or library. You will find a plethora of topics and information by a variety of experts. Here is the list of nonfiction subjects at Barnes & Noble:

Activity & Game Books
Antiques & Collectibles
Art, Architecture & Photography
Bibles & Christianity
Biography
Business Books
Computers
Cookbooks, Food & Wine
Crafts & Hobbies
Current Affairs & Politics
Diet, Health & Fitness
Education
Engineering
Foreign Languages
History
Home & Garden
Humor
Law
Medicine & Nursing Books
Music, Film & Performing Arts
Nature
New Age & Alternative Beliefs
Parenting & Family
Pets
Philosophy
Psychology
Reference
Religion
Role-Playing & Fantasy Games
Science & Technology
Self-Help & Relationships
Social Sciences
Sports
Study Aids & Test Prep
Transportation
Travel
True Crime
Weddings

Within all of these subjects, authors were able to compile enough information to create an entire book. So there should be many ways to break one of these topics down into different articles with different slants. You can also take a look at the authors. They are clearly experts in their fields. Look them up to learn more about them. Maybe they have an interesting backstory that would make a good profile, or maybe you could include them as experts in a piece. You can also look for elements of a topic that don't seem to be covered or viewpoints that are underrepresented.

INTERNET

The wealth of information, stories, news, photos and, of course, cat videos on the Web can be overwhelming. But it is a great source for mining ideas. Think of some topics you are interested in writing about. Maybe even use some of the ideas from the earlier chart. Set a timer for one hour. See what sites show up first and who shows up as the experts. Click on the links to see where they take you. Look for interesting information, facts, or people who could potentially make a good article. Keep track of these ideas along the way since we all know how easy it is to get lost on the Internet.

TELEVISION

Some say watching television or movies is a waste of time, but not if you are searching for potential ideas. How-to shows, such as those on the Home and Garden Television (HGTV) and talk shows, seem like the obvious first choices since they cover a variety of topics and projects that could lend themselves well to articles. But weekly sitcoms and dramas can also spark many ideas.

I recently watched an episode of a sitcom that dealt with the different ways men and women argue. For the men it was more physical, then it was over. The women took a more passive-aggressive approach. Yes, the television show played up stereotypes, but some potential article ideas surfaced. The obvious one is the different ways men and women communicate with those of the opposite gender and those of the same gender. Another could address stereotypes and how they come to be, or one could offer tips to manage conflict with your best friend. Whether it is with a drama or comedy, television is great at highlighting the challenges, issues, and situations of daily life, and these all have the potential to make interesting articles.

FINDING YOUR ANGLE

Once you open your eyes and your mind, you will find ideas everywhere. But keep in mind there are really no new ideas. If you visit a newsstand in January and look at all the covers of women's magazines, you will see some common themes: weight loss, diets, and exercise. Here are some actual cover lines from January issues:

- Bye-Bye Belly! 3 New Easy Ways to Lose It
- Eat More, Weigh Less: Snacks that Slim You Down
- Strong & Hot Toned Arms, Flat Abs: The Best New Workout

So if there are no new ideas, what are you supposed to do? The key is to find a new slant, a new way to say the same thing.

At first it may seem daunting to find a unique approach to an idea. But freelance writer Jordan Rosenfeld says don't doubt your ideas. "I can't tell you how many times I've done that only to see *my* idea published by someone else. Try to look at any idea through multiple lenses. What's the business angle, the personal angle, the environmental angle, the consumer angle, and so on?"

Here are different ways to find new angles on a topic that will catch the attention of an editor.

Opposites

One way to come up with a fresh idea is to think of opposites. If January is all about weight loss and diets, an article about losing weight without dieting could be a different take on this. Years ago, I took a trip to Las Vegas for few days to do what most people do in this city, gamble. While sitting at a slot machine in the hope of winning millions, I wondered what people would do in Vegas if they didn't want to gamble or had used up all their money (which I was close to doing). The thought interested me, and it hung on. I paid more attention to the other activities in the city and other ways people could spend their time instead of gambling. When I got home, I continued to research this topic and found quite a few activities to do besides spending money at a blackjack table. I sent off a query for "25 Things to Do in Las Vegas When You Don't Want to Gamble" to *Highroads* magazine and got the assignment.

Go Small

Some topics feel overwhelming and huge. A travel piece about all of New York City might seem like a big undertaking because it is. But if you can take this topic and look for smaller ideas, it will be more manageable. Picking one Manhattan neighborhood to write about would be easier. If you look back at the January cover line examples, you will see this is how these topics were addressed. The first one, "Bye-Bye Belly! 3 New Easy Ways to Lose It," didn't focus on the overall idea of becoming healthy because that is a big topic to tackle. Instead, this article only focused on the belly.

Go Big

Another way is to take one topic, research it, and find out as much as you can. A roundup style article is perfect for this "Go Big" approach. Here are some examples from magazines:

- 35 Irresistible Summer Recipes
- 75 Crazy Hot Sex Moves
- Women Writing About the Wild: 25 Essential Authors

The writers for these articles took one basic idea and found as much as they could about the topics and put them into one piece full of bite-sized information.

Quest

Quests are an intriguing way to write about a topic. They work for a variety of ideas, especially travel articles. Instead of writing a standard travel destination piece, create a quest. Write about searching for something or someone. The main focus becomes the story while the destination becomes the setting. It allows the travel information to be woven in more organically. Travel writer Andrew McCarthy does this with many of his articles for *National Geographic Traveler.* One piece, "Chasing the Black Pearl," was about his quest in Tahiti to find one of these unique pearls as a gift for his mother. Another one, "Steeped in Darjeeling," shared his search for the best cup of tea in this region. In both cases he told the story while giving interesting facts and history about the place as well as painting vivid pictures of the area and the people living there.

A quest works in other realms as well: the quest for the perfect chocolate chip cookie recipe, the quest for the best deal on home furnishings, the quest for the best way to handle conflict with your teenager.

Here is an interview I did with McCarthy where he shares tips about travel writing and talks more about creating a quest as an article focus.

Article Example: Service Piece

3 TIPS TO IMPROVE YOUR TRAVEL WRITING

Actor, director, and travel writer Andrew McCarthy shares insights and tips about his newest career.

By Kerrie Flanagan

Best known for his roles in 1980s' classics, like *Pretty in Pink* and *Weekend at Bernie's*, Andrew McCarthy is not one of those celebrities dabbling in writing; he is a writer who happens to be a celebrity. Since his first published article in *National Geographic Traveler* in 2006, to being named Travel Journalist of the Year by the Society of American Travel Writers in 2010, to the release of his best-selling memoir *The Longest Way Home* in 2012, McCarthy has shown and continues to show his talent as a writer.

Ten years prior to the publishing of his first article, he traveled the world and filled notebooks with anecdotes. As he read travel magazines, he found they weren't capturing that deep, transformative connection he experienced from his trips. Someone suggested he write professionally about his travels. A friend put him in touch with the editor of *National Geographic Traveler*. When the two met and McCarthy asked to write for the magazine, the editor said, "You're an actor." McCarthy replied, "Yes, but I know how to tell a story." After a year of e-mails and badgering from McCarthy, the editor finally agreed and sent him on assignment to Ireland.

For McCarthy, travel profoundly affected his life, and that is the undercurrent in everything he writes. He is grateful to have found writing at this point in his life. Like his acting and directing, writing makes him feel like himself and taps into the core of who he is. He believes "It is our job as writers to do the work, have the courage to bring it out and to present it to the world, because that's why we are here."

FIND YOUR LEAD IN THE SMALL DETAILS

Tiny details and incidents capture the essence of a place, believes McCarthy. "Once you find that nugget you can hang the whole story on it," says McCarthy, "and the rest is basically arranging furniture." You follow the lede with a nut graph, three or four supporting examples, and then circle back to the lede at the end.

On a recent assignment McCarthy struggled to find his lede. "I was in Seville and I had wonderful vignettes that I was going to put in the story about bullfighting, about flamenco, but I didn't know what the story was. ... I still needed to find the thread to give the story any kind of purpose." He began to notice a picture of a Virgin Mary statue crying crystal tears in every restaurant he visited, and then went on a quest to find the actual statue.

"Often I am looking for a lede, and I can't see it. I'd seen the picture of the Virgin Mary twenty times before I realized, 'wait a minute-that's Seville.' ... It's laced in history, it's mysterious, and those were all the things that Seville was to me."

In 2011 he wrote a story, "Courting Vienna," for *National Geographic Traveler*. His purpose for the article was to go to Vienna and live as local a life as possible. He hung the whole story on a one-sentence conversation he had with a waitress. "I had gone to that coffee shop every day while I was there and she waited on me every day. ... Finally, one day I asked, 'How long have you worked here?' She said, 'Too long.'" She became the lede to his article, which ended up focusing on Viennese coffeehouses. "It wasn't just about some grumpy waitress. It captured something about the whole culture. Those coffeehouses and what life is like; how you endure."

Small, specific details like these give an article depth. A good lede becomes the thread, giving the story purpose and taking it beyond a travelogue.

GET OUT AND EXPLORE THE PLACE YOU'RE WRITING ABOUT

The best way to learn about a place is to get out of the hotel room as soon as you arrive, walk around, get lost a little, and pay attention to details. "Walking gives you a rhythm in a place, and you need to begin to understand the rhythm so you're not an outsider." He believes asking for help is a good way to connect with people and begin to learn more about where you are.

A good travel writer seeks out the unique aspects of an area in order to portray a more complete picture to the reader, more from a local point of view instead of as a tourist.

McCarthy always carries a notebook with him, but he writes down more than just a travelogue of where he has been and what he has seen. He writes down his feelings about a place, anecdotes, vignettes, scenes, and moments that capture his experience of a place. "Getting quotes from taxi drivers shows me a lazy travel writer, and I stop reading." Facts, he says, he can get later.

There are days he takes copious notes, and other days pass with nothing. Often toward the end of a trip he does exactly what he did when he arrived, he walks around. "Lines, phrases, entire paragraphs will come up, and I will stop where I am and write them down; often they end up in that form in the final draft. It's important not to start writing too early in the process, but when it wants to start coming, you have to be open to it."

TELL A STORY, DON'T SELL A DESTINATION

One of the reason's McCarthy feels he has found success in travel writing is because he approaches it from a story-first point of view. He says one of the biggest mistakes travel writers make is they write about destinations. Storytelling grabs people. "It is how we communicate, and that is how we should approach travel writing."

Good travel writing is about being curious and being willing to do the work to dig beneath the surface to uncover the real undercurrent of a place and find that story. Go beyond writing descriptions about what you see, the hours a place is open, or a list of the tourist attractions. Find that great lede, then add dialogue and scenes in order to take readers along on the journey.

He finds quest stories great because there is always a good hook like when he went searching for the perfect cup of tea in Darjeeling, India. Readers enjoy these because there is an interesting story. As a writer, you have a clear direction making it easier to go out into the field to find evidence of it.

For instance, McCarthy wanted to write about Tahiti, but he needed more of an angle to pitch to the editor than the destination. After some initial research, he found that 95 percent of all black pearls come from Tahiti. Because his mother had a big birthday coming up, he combined the two ideas and went on a quest to Tahiti to find a pearl farmer who would let him dive into the water, pluck an oyster from its bed, and bring home a black pearl for his mom.

That became the story for the article, "In Search of the Black Pearl," for the October 2010 issue of *National Geographic Traveler*. His quest for the pearl draws readers in and keeps them engaged until the end, while facts about black pearls, Tahiti, and even dolphins are seamlessly woven throughout the article. He could have easily written a destination piece about Tahiti, with lots of interesting facts about the location, including the pearls, but by making it a story with a beginning, middle, and end, he created something that taps into the core of the readers and connects with them on an emotional level.

DEVELOPING IDEAS WITHIN A TOPIC

An idea map is a great visual tool to help you take a big topic or idea and break it down into smaller, more focused article ideas. You can do this with a regular piece of notebook paper, but I suggest you get creative. Find a bigger piece of paper and some colored pencils or markers. Then clear a table so you can spread out.

Draw a circle in the middle of the paper. In that space, put a broad topic, for example, chocolate. This is a big topic and one everyone is familiar with. If you were to pitch an article about chocolate to an editor, it would get rejected; it's too broad of a topic. Now draw other circles with topics based on the broad subject of chocolate and put a connecting line to the big circle. For example, in one smaller circle you can put *history*. Then some offshoots of that could include:

- Chocolate in ancient civilizations
- Hershey's, the early years
- Introduction of chocolate in the United States

For chocolate in ancient civilizations, you can even break off into smaller circles with specific civilizations like the Aztec and the Maya.

Another circle could be for angles geared toward children's magazines:

- Tour of a chocolate factory
- An interview with a chocolate maker
- How are chocolate Easter bunnies made?

Another could be health topics:

- Benefits of dark chocolate
- Which chocolate is the healthiest?
- Does milk chocolate have any health benefits?
- Chocolate's effect on libido

Get as creative as possible and go as deep as you can into a subject. Refer to the chart from earlier in the chapter for ideas. Put as many circles as possible relating to one topic. By the time you are finished you will have numerous ideas to pitch to an editor, and you will have detailed information to include in the article should you get the assignment.

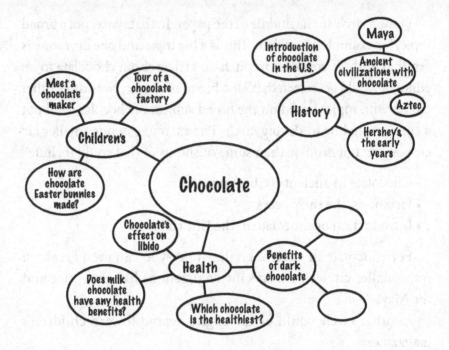

Creating the perfect slant for an idea takes practice, but it is an important skill to master. By paying attention to the world around you, the events in your life and the experiences you or others may have, you will begin to recognize great ideas and be able to mold them into great pitches.

Once you come up with an idea, how do you know it is going to be a good one? Freelance writer Tom Keer says the only good way to vet an idea is to subject it to time. "Good ideas withstand the test of time while other ones reveal themselves as a passing fancy. By time I don't mean a decade. In some instances, it might be an hour or two. During that hour or two your mood will change, and when it does you'll return to review that idea and see if it's any good. In many instances, I use context disorientation to rapidly shift my frame of reference. I get out of the office and take my dogs for a walk. I flirt with my wife over lunch. I might go fishing for a while. What happens when I return to my desk is that I look at the same material from a different perspective."

Article Example: Roundup

10 WAYS TO COLLECT YOUR IDEAS

Ideas are the staple of every writer's repertoire and because of this you want to find an effective way to collect and store these ideas. There are many ways to save your thoughts. It may take some trial and error before you land on the one that works best for you.

1. Idea Folder

Use a folder to house items that interest you: a fascinating new store that opened in your area, intriguing places you travel, a national park with interesting facts, or a unique festival coming to your city. Cut out the articles and put them in your file.

2. Digital Recorder

If you are more of an audio person, a recorder (or your phone or a separate device) allows you to verbally make a quick note of an idea or topic. Once or twice a week listen to your recordings to see if there is anything you want to pursue.

3. Spreadsheet

A spreadsheet allows you to sort your data and information by things like topic, potential magazines, or timeliness. You can use a notebook or recorder to initially capture your ideas and thoughts, then add the ideas to your spreadsheet. Or you can house your spreadsheet on a Cloud server like Google Drive and add ideas from your phone or tablet.

4. Three-Ring Binder

Are you a little more hands on, yet you need something a little more organized than just a hanging folder stuffed with ideas? Get a three-ring binder. Create different sections with tabbed dividers based on the topics you want to focus on. In each section have notebook paper to write your ideas and clear page protectors for photos, brochures, notes, or other interesting items.

5. Pinterest

For those visual writers, Pinterest is a great way to organize your ideas in one place. Create a collection of boards based on different topics. As you peruse the Internet and find interesting stories, photos and articles, save (pin) the images associated with them to your Pinterest board/s.

6. Spiral Notebook

Looking for a simple way to keep a running record of your ideas? Get a spiral notebook. You can get a small one to keep with you all the time and/or have one at your writing space that you can add to as ideas pop into your head.

7. Whiteboard

Do you like to see all the potential ideas you have found and refer to them often? Hang up a whiteboard near your writing space. You can create organized, color-coded lists based on publications or topics. When your board gets full or you want to start over, take a photo of it and create a folder on your computer to save the image.

8. Idea Jar

Set up a jar to collect your ideas. Have small pieces of paper near it and keep some with you when you are not at home. When an idea hits, write it down and put it in the jar. When you have some writing time, reach into the jar and create a query based on that idea.

9. Notecards

Notecards are versatile. You can use all white or color coded. You can store them in a container with dividers or hole punch them and arrange them on a circular key ring. When it's time to write, lay them out to see all your ideas.

10. Phone Apps

We have so much technology at our fingertips. If you carry your phone all the time, finding an app to store your ideas may be the easiest option for you. Here are two options.

Article Example: Review

EVERNOTE AND TRELLO

1. Evernote

This powerful note-taking tool helps writers collect and organize various types of notes including text, screenshots, photos, sketches, voice memos, and more. The information can be accessed and added through a program on your computer or through a smartphone app.

Evernote is great for collecting information and research for articles. Create a notebook for the article, then fill it with pertinent information. The Evernote extension for your computer allows you to save articles, photos, or other resources from the Internet directly into your notebook. The app can be used to take a photo, type a note, or add a voice note on the go. The recorder feature can be used to record interviews that can be saved to the notebook. Both the phone app and program on your computer will sync the information. You also have the ability to tag your notes for an easy search later.

If working on a collaborative project, you can share notes and folders with other people. There is even a chat feature that allows you to converse with others about the information.

Evernote is available to use on or offline, which is a plus if you are in areas without Internet or a network. It is a handy program that is worth checking out.

2. Trello

Trello is fantastic for organizing projects and timelines. You can jot down notes in Trello, but its real strength is in creating a workflow or project. It can also be used on your computer or with the smartphone app.

Trello is a visually based system of cards and lists. Each card contains lots of details including checklists, comments, descriptions, and file attachments that can be organized into lists. There is even a feature to add color labels. You can create lists of different publications, and each card can be a different idea you want to pitch. You can create a list of people to interview for an assignment, along with the information you want to include in each section of the article, and helpful resources. You can track where submissions are in the process. Each card can be easily moved to another list by clicking and dragging it to a new spot. You can also share your lists with others on a collaborative project.

Trello also has power-ups. The calendar one is especially useful for writers. It provides you with a great visual of upcoming deadlines or necessary follow-ups. A downside to the program is that you have to be connected to the Internet to use it.

COMBINED POWER

If you are having a hard time deciding between the two programs, there is a way to use them together. Trello has an Evernote Power-Up that allows you to combine the amazing features of both. Jot down your notes and ideas in Evernote, and when you are in Trello, you can attach the appropriate notes to the right Trello card. Now you have all your information in one convenient location.

HOW THE PROS DO IT

FREELANCE WRITERS SHARE HOW THEY ORGANIZE THEIR IDEAS

JORDAN ROSENFELD: I am incredibly old school. I keep a paper week-by-week calendar and chart everything on paper. Otherwise I might use old-fashioned spreadsheets and lists. But I have tried and failed to adapt to new technologies.

DANIELLE BRAFF: I write a daily to-do list. I also have a list of stories to write, which is separate, so that I never forget to write stories (that's a huge fear for me). I have separate notebooks for both.

MEGAN HILL: I refuse to use anything too fancy. There are tons of apps and websites out there for organizing ideas, but I use good old-fashioned spreadsheets.

ROXANNE HAWN: I keep a separate folder in my e-mail in-box for information I think I might use later or may spur an idea. I also keep scribbled notes to myself in a special file folder so when I'm casting about for the next thing to write, I have a place to review kernels of ideas I've jotted down.

STACEY MCKENNA: For my first year I used a spreadsheet. Now I use Trello. I've got "pitch cards" (with checklists of whom I've pitched, due dates, labels, and other info) that I move between folders based on their status (e.g., pitched, waiting to hear from editor, negotiating rates, assigned, editor editing, etc.).

DEBBIE HANSON: I generally use Google Drive to organize a running list of ideas or potential topics.

MICKEY GOODMAN: Busted! I don't have a real system. When my head is buzzing with an idea (even during the night), I get up and jot it down. Sometimes the ideas are winners; other times they're totally nonstories. I brainstorm outlets for the winners and keep a running list. Before sending a query I do some research, talk with people I want to interview to see if they are willing, then query several publications simultaneously. Caution: Take care to personalize each query with an angle that fits their editorial calendar (usually available online), and make sure to address it to a particular editor.

AMANDA CASTLEMAN: I keep lists of story ideas on my phone, laptop, and a palm-sized, spiral-top notebook in my purse. Accessibility remains key—I like to record inspirations while they're fresh, anywhere and anytime. ... I'm such a fan of old-school notebooks. Pads of paper never need recharging, and they don't get targeted by random thieves. Win!

TOOLS FOR ORGANIZING INFORMATION

Pocket
Allows you to save articles, videos, and other interesting content from the Web in one location to read later. Content can be viewed offline.
www.getpocket.com

Evernote
A program for taking, storing and sharing notes.
www.evernote.com

Trello
Organizes projects into boards with cards and lists.
www.trello.com

ORGANIZE THOUGHTS WITH THESE MINDMAPPING TOOLS

Bubbl.us
    www.bubbl.us
MindNode
    www.mindnode.com
Mindly
    www.mindlyapp.com
MindMeister
    www.mindmeister.com

CHAPTER THREE

STUDYING A MAGAZINE

There is one piece of advice I give new freelance magazine writers all the time: Study the magazines you are interested in pitching. I can't say this enough, so I will say it once more—read and study the magazines you want to query. Investing time upfront to learn all you can about a publication will lead to more success in the long run. You'll pitch stories that fit the magazine, and editors will appreciate the time and effort you took to understand their magazine. Editors have the task of putting together content and overseeing photos and graphics, all targeted for a specific readership. The more you learn about the reader, the style and tone of the magazine's content, and the types of articles they publish, the more you will understand the overall goal and direction of the publication. This will allow you to target your queries to the specific audience. You will also avoid wasting time—yours and the editor's—with queries that aren't a match.

Robbin Gould, editor for *Family Motor Coaching* magazine, wants writers to understand this point. "Please know your market! The more familiar you are with a magazine's unique requirements, the better you can tailor your articles to that publication. You will be successful, and your editor will be happy."

Jonah Ogles, editor for *Outside*, echoes this sentiment. "I wish more writers would read the magazine and site before querying. I never hold it against writers for pitching things we've covered before (who can keep up with every outlet they're pitching?), but I often get ideas that are so far from the type of thing we cover that I question if they even meant to send the pitch to me." He encourages writers to focus on a half dozen publications and understand those magazines inside and out.

Become a connoisseur of magazines. Look through them whenever you get a chance—at the doctor's office, at the hairdresser, or while you are in line at the grocery store. Check out newsstands where you will find a wide variety of publications. Keep magazines in your car for when you are waiting for your kids to get out of school or are meeting a friend who is running late. Be on the lookout for free publications you can take home; many communities have them. And don't forget about airline magazines—they are free for the taking.

Digital versions of your favorite periodicals come in handy when all you have is your phone or tablet with you. Do you have a library card? RBdigital has an app associated with many libraries that allows you to check out and read digital versions of a wide variety of magazines.

The bottom line? Immerse yourself in the world of magazines and learn all you can about as many different ones as possible.

There are five key components to understand before you pitch an editor:

- the reader
- the style
- the types of articles
- the writer's guidelines
- what articles have recently been published

KNOW THE READER

Every magazine has a certain readership: teenage girl, budget traveler, mother of young children, and so on. It is imperative you know as much about that reader as you can before submitting a query to the editor. The more you know about who reads the magazine, the more you can tailor your query, article, or essay to best reach that audience.

How can you find the target audience for a specific magazine? The key is in the advertising. Companies spend thousands of dollars getting their messages out to their consumers. They invest in magazines directed at their target market. You can learn a lot about the reader by paying attention to the ads in a publication, and this goes for online magazines too. What are the ages of the people in the ads? Are they families? Singles? What types of products are highlighted? Expensive clothes? Organic foods? Luxury cars and world travel, or family cars and domestic travel?

Here are some of the ads in a summer issue of *Backpacker* magazine:

- Insect repellent: Image shows a woman hiking through the woods.
- Pickup truck: Image shows the truck next to a couple in their thirties by their tent in the mountains.
- Beer: There are a couple of beer ads. One shows two men and two women kayaking on a mountain lake, and the other shows two men and two women at a picnic table by a lake with a canoe on the shore.
- Solar watch (includes a compass, barometer, and altimeter): Image shows a man and a woman with backpacks and hiking gear crossing a river on a log.

- Destinations: There are many ads for destinations, and they tend to show more rugged, extreme activities; both men and women are in the ads.
- Gear (backpacks, shoes, coats): Images tend to show gear being used for mountain climbing, camping in the backwoods, and hiking rough terrain.

Based on these ads, this magazine is not for a casual recreationist. It is geared for those who enjoy a more rugged, extreme outdoor experience. Both men and women around their late thirties and forties were in the ads, and the gear featured is high quality, high cost. These readers are serious about the outdoors, and they have money to spend on it.

In contrast, these were some of the ads found in a spring issue of *Travel + Leisure*:

- Car (full-size SUV): Image shows two couples wearing suits, dresses, and heels outside an opera house.
- High-end purse: Image is of a woman in a white summer dress by the ocean with her purse.
- Upscale cruise line: Image shows a middle-aged couple wearing nice clothes for an evening out, standing on the balcony of a cruise ship and drinking champagne.
- Wine club: Image shows a beautiful tray of wine, cheese, and crackers by a vineyard.
- Chocolate: Image has a woman in a silky nightgown sitting on a chair eating chocolate at night. Her window overlooks the Golden Gate Bridge.

By looking at the advertisements, we can see the target audience for *Travel + Leisure* is clearly different from *Backpacker*. *Travel + Leisure* focuses on luxury travel for affluent people with a considerable amount of disposable income. These readers fly first class and enjoy five-star vacations. *Backpacker* readers also have disposable income, but their idea of fun is outdoor adventures. They are interested in pushing themselves physically through intense hikes and backpacking or camping off the beaten path. Both of these readerships have disposable income, yet their choices on how to spend that money differ. Through the ads you can understand what is important to each of these readers before sending a pitch to the editor.

Another way to find out the demographics of the reader is to locate the media kit on the magazine's website. This document provides information about the readership to potential advertisers, but it is a gold mine for freelance writers. The media kit provides information like average age, income, gender, hobbies, education, home ownership, and marital status. It is usually found at the very bottom of the magazine's website where you typically find the About Us information. Sometimes it will say Media Kit; other times you must click on the link for Advertising.

Looking up the media kits for *Travel + Leisure* and *Backpacker* confirmed what was already apparent in the ads. *Travel + Leisure*'s median reader age is 52, the median household income is $101,639, 71 percent are married, and 75 percent own their own home. *Backpacker*'s average age is 40, the median household income is $81,839, and 80 percent graduated from college.

This becomes invaluable when looking at ideas and topics to pitch to a magazine. For instance, in the media kit for *5280* magazine, 66 percent of the readers are married, 86 percent own their own home, and their median income is $287,076. Pitching an article on where to find the best deals on apartments in Denver is definitely not a good fit for *5280* since a majority of the readers own their own home. An article on the best bars in Denver to meet other singles is also not a good idea. But one about the most romantic mountain weekend getaways in Colorado to take your spouse is a possibility. In addition to the basic demographics of age, education, and income, the media kit revealed that 96 percent of its readers plan to visit a mountain town in the next year. So knowing the majority of readers are married, have disposable income and plan to visit a resort makes this article idea feasible for this publication.

KNOW THE STYLE

Each magazine has its own style and tone. It's what makes the difference between *The New Yorker* and *Time* magazine. Some magazines are very literary, some are more conversational, while others are more informational. It is important to read and study the articles in the magazines to have a good understanding of their style.

When I worked on my first assignment for *Alaska* magazine, I printed off articles from back issues. Using colored pencils, I underlined quotes from experts, facts, dialogue, and description. I used this information to help me understand what the editor expects and to be clear about the style and tone of the publication.

Below are two excerpts from travel articles that are about road trips. Read over each selection. Pay attention to

- the use of quotes
- the point of view (first-person, third-person ...)
- the descriptions
- the overall tone of the article

THE BEAUTIFUL BERKSHIRES

Family Motor Coaching magazine July 2016
By Anna Lee Braunstein

Grandeur inside and out is featured at The Mount, the home of writer Edith Wharton, in Lenox. Bejeweled in the spring, lush green in the summer, and ablaze with reds, oranges, and yellows in the fall, western Massachusetts is a must-see destination for nature lovers. But it has even more to offer: art, history, theater, and music. A drive along the north-south U.S. Route 7 will enchant, entertain, and educate visitors to the Berkshires region. It's typically snowy in winter but abuzz from spring through fall with an abundance of activities. This drive through the Berkshires begins at Great Barrington, at the junction of U.S. 7 and State Route 23, and meanders north along U.S. 7 to the Vermont border.

GREAT BARRINGTON

Back in 1967, Arlo Guthrie sang about Alice's Restaurant. People wanted to know if it was a real place. Well, the lyrics explain that Alice didn't live in a restaurant. She lived in the church near the restaurant. If you visit Great Barrington, you can find it—Trinity Church, built in 1829 as St. James Chapel. Today, Old Trinity Church is home to the Guthrie Center.

Ray and Alice Brock, who worked at a private school in town, purchased the church in 1964. They befriended local students who appreciated their outlook on life, and Guthrie was one of them. In 1991 he purchased the building and established the Guthrie Center, where the Troubadour music series (folk, rock, and bluegrass) is presented. Hootenanny shows are offered each Thursday night. For the concert schedule and more information, visit www .guthriecenter.org.

STOCKBRIDGE

The most famous artist of the Berkshires is Norman Rockwell, whose depiction of everyday life in America made him popular and beloved. The Norman Rockwell Museum displays the largest collection of his wonderful paintings. His final studio, formerly located in the backyard of his Stockbridge home, was moved to the museum grounds in 1986.

Often criticized for being "just an illustrator," Rockwell was proud of his chosen field. His art reflected the charm, simplicity, and humor that are traits of Americana. He described his work in these words: "Without thinking too much about it in specific terms, I was showing the America I knew and observed to others who might not have noticed."

At nineteen he became art editor of the magazine of the Boy Scouts of America, *Boys' Life*. At twenty-two he painted his first cover for *The Saturday Evening Post*, a magazine he regarded as the "greatest show window in America." In 1943, the *Post* published his most famous work, "The Four Freedoms," over a four-week period. His relationship with *The Post* lasted forty-seven years and included 323 covers.

In 1963 Rockwell went to work for *Look* magazine and presented his views on the positive and negative aspects of American life for the next ten years. "The Problem We All Live With," his depiction of a black family moving into a white neighborhood, depicts both the tension and the hope that integration offered.

Visitors can study and appreciate the work of this important artist in the museum gallery building designed by Robert A.M. Stern, the architect who also designed the George W. Bush Presidential Library and Museum. Just steps from the visitors' desk, in a room of their own, are the full-size paintings of "The Four Freedoms." These inspiring paintings set the tone for viewing more of his work.

Visitors can take in free orientation talks. Audio tours narrated by Norman's son Peter Rockwell are available for rent. On the lower floor of the museum is ArtZone, a collection of all of the *Post* covers. The terrace café is a pleasant place to get a bite to eat. Bronze and stone sculptures by Peter are interspersed throughout the grounds.

Up a path from the museum stands Norman Rockwell's studio, shown as if he were still at work. It depicts a day in October 1960 when he was working on his painting "Golden Rule." His easel and paintbrushes at the ready, all that's missing is the man who created the iconic works. To learn more, go to www.nrm.org.

CHASING WATERFALLS

Sunset magazine February 2014
By Mac McClelland

Jumping the guardrail to get a better look at Hamma Hamma Falls doesn't seem like a bad idea, at first. Not until we reach the edge of the mossy outcroppings above it and we, too, seem likely to tumble into the cerulean plunge pool do I consider that the weak sapling I'm grasping is my only safeguard against falling to my death. Or that my husband is perched on a 75-foot cliff covered in slippery flora. It's then that I wonder: Why are we risking our lives for this?

The water does roar. It does rush big and hard and beautifully, sucking all the energy of the surrounding gorge into its vortex, leaving a rare stillness in the space. But we did just see another waterfall, with a 125-foot drop, an hour ago. And over the past two days, eight more before that. Also, we're going to see three more this afternoon.

It was my sister who had beckoned us to Washington's Olympic Peninsula, a mass of thick green beauty to the west of Puget Sound, all glittering straits and canals and ocean on the sides and temperate rain forest in the middle. Since she moved here a year ago, she's been swearing that the area's scenery rivals that of any place in the country. It was the Olympic Peninsula Waterfall Trail that cemented my interest in fact-checking her claims.

The idea of the trail was conceived six years ago when the visitor bureau realized there are at least 26 cascades spread all around the Olympic Peninsula's 5,316 square miles. It hasn't been well publicized, but that doesn't deter people who walk into the area's visitor centers: "We can't keep the brochures on the rack," an assistant told me over the phone.

A few weeks later, my husband and I had multiple copies of said brochure, plus a slew of maps, spread across the bedsheets of the Ravenscroft Inn in Port Townsend. The city of 9,000 two hours northwest of Seattle—with the lightly heartbreaking slogan "One of the coolest small towns in America"—served as our gateway to the lost-world remoteness of Olympic National Park. In the newly renovated B&B, we plotted our course. The waterfall trail isn't meant to be done in one trip, as it would take several weeks and criminal amounts of gas, but we resolved to cover three of its seven legs, thirteen waterfalls, in three days.

Like most sentient beings, my husband and I love waterfalls. Together, we've trekked to the end of many a long trail to witness even a sad little summer trickle along a rock face. In the year-round wetness of the Olympic Peninsula—where even the comparatively dry areas get 20 inches of rain a year, and where the rivers and creeks of Olympic National Park swell with precipitation that can top 180 inches a year—I wondered if our wonderment might abate and we'd start taking them for granted. And yet even at the outset, each one we chose to skip felt like an opportunity missed.

"What if it's beautiful?" we asked each other when we reluctantly decided Striped Peak Falls was too far out of our way. We knew plenty of the others would also be beautiful. But: "What if it's the most beautiful?"

The next morning, we set off west on U.S. 101 across the peninsula, starting a loop around the outside edge of the park that would end at my sister's place south of Port Townsend. Several dozen miles of mostly empty roads later, we arrived at our first waterfall. I was instantly sure this one would be the most beautiful.

Some of the falls on the trail are visible right from the road. One of them sits behind a hike that is 13 miles each way. This first one required parking and walking a 200-foot paved trail, and then there it was, in the clearing, almost close enough to touch: Madison Creek Falls. She was loud. She was complex, descending into countless streams that united as one stream through the surrounding greenery. She was breathtaking, as in, we were taking deeper breaths.

***

Let's take a closer look at these two travel articles. The first one is from *Family Motor Coaching* magazine, a trade publication for RV enthusiasts who are members of the Family Motor Coaching Association. Written in a third-person point of view, the article provides great information and facts about traveling to the Berkshires in western Massachusetts. It opens with a brief visual of the area, then mentions the region offers art, history, theater, and music. It goes on to highlight different attractions in the area, with a brief history of each along with information about tours and websites for further reference. Travel articles like this one are written with an informative tone and are intended for readers to enjoy, then visit the places highlighted in the piece.

The second example is from *Sunset* magazine, a lifestyle magazine dedicated to readers in the western part of the United States. This article is written in a first-person point of view and shares the writer's experience with readers. The tone is more personal and conversational, allowing readers to feel as though they are there with the writer. But it also weaves in interesting facts about the area and other pertinent information for those who may want to visit the waterfalls.

Let's dive into them deeper. In this chart, we will look at how each article uses facts, description, quotes, and travel/visitor information.

	THE BEAUTIFUL BERKSHIRES	CHASING WATERFALLS
FACTS	• 1967, Arlo Guthrie sang about Alice's Restaurant • Trinity Church built in 1829 • Ray & Alice Brock purchased the church in 1964 • 1991, Guthrie purchased the building and established the Guthrie Center • Norman Rockwell's studio moved to the museum grounds in 1986 • At 19 Rockwell became the editor of *Boys' Life* • At 22 he painted his first cover for *Saturday Evening Post* • 1943, published The Four Freedoms • His relationship with the *Post* lasted 47 years and included 323 covers • 1963, Rockwell went to work for *Look* magazine	• 75-foot cliff • 125-foot drop • Trail conceived 6 years ago • At least 26 cascades • Spread around the Olympic Peninsula's 5316 Square Miles • City of 9,000, 2 hours northwest of Seattle • The Olympic Peninsula gets 20 inches of rain a year • Rivers and creeks of Olympic National Park swell with precipitation that can top 180 inches a year

DESCRIPTION	• Lush green • Ablaze with reds, oranges and yellows in the fall	• Mossy outcroppings • Cerulean plunge pool • Slippery flora • The water does roar • It rushes big and hard and beautiful, sucking all the energy of the surrounding gorge into its vortex • Stillness in the space • A mass of thick green beauty • Glittering straits • She was loud. She was complex, descending into countless streams that united as one stream through the surrounding greenery. • She was breathtaking, as in, we were taking deeper breaths.
TRAVEL/ VISITOR INFORMATION	• Great Barrington, at the junction of U.S. 7 and State Route 23 • Meanders north along U.S. 7 to the Vermont border • Hootenannies every Thursday night • Norman Rockwell Museum displays largest collection of Rockwell's paintings • Visitors can study and appreciate his work in the Museum Gallery • A number of steps from the visitor's desk are the Four Freedoms paintings • Visitors can take in free orientation talks • Terrace café is a pleasant place to get a bite to eat • Up the path is Norman Rockwell's studio • Website information	• We set off west on U.S. 101 across the peninsula, starting a loop around the outside edge of the park • 200-foot walking trail to Madison Creek Falls
QUOTES	• Indirect quote from Rockwell at the museum	

These are well-done travel articles, but each is unique in its style and tone and was written with a certain publication and readership in mind. You can see they both have a good number of facts. Where they differ most is with description and travel/visitor information.

The Berkshires article includes lots of specific information for readers who may want to visit these sites. The waterfall article has some, but not nearly as many. On the other hand, the waterfall article weaves in many beautiful descriptions to paint the scene.

KNOW THE TYPES OF ARTICLES

In the magazine world there are some general types of articles. Not all articles fit into a specific category, but if yours does, it is good to mention it in your pitch (which I will cover more in depth at the end of this chapter). It gives the editor a clear idea of the kind of article you are suggesting and where it might fit best in the magazine. Here are the main ones.

Front of Book (FOB)

Front-of-the-book pieces usually follow the masthead. (This is the list of staff found within the first few pages of the magazine.) Front of the book is industry talk for the front section of the magazine. They are shorter articles and can be everything from product reviews to short interviews to news items. *Family Circle* always has a big front-of-the-book section. In one issue there was a short article about healthy soups that included three recipes. It was about 350 words of text. *National Geographic Traveler* has a variety of FOBs that vary in length. For example, there was a short piece of sixty words sharing about *guayusa* tea from the Amazon, and a little longer article of 250 words about elves in Reykjavik, Iceland. Editors typically have a hard time finding writers to submit FOBs because most writers want the big features. They tend to forget the editors need shorter pieces too, so these are a great way to break into a new magazine.

Roundup

Like a cowboy rounding up his cattle into one location, a roundup focuses on one topic. A variety of ideas are rounded up and presented in one article, for example, "10 Best Water Parks in the United States" or "15 Non-Electronic Ideas to Keep Your Kids Entertained on a Road Trip." Roundups are typically informative pieces sharing insights and resources about a certain topic. The basic format of these articles is simple with short tidbits about each of the highlighted subcategories. But they tend to involve a lot of legwork and research to get all the information for each section.

Listicle

Typically found online, a *listicle* is a term used to describe any article written in the form of a list. Listicles were made popular by websites like BuzzFeed and Bustle. It is similar to a roundup in that you are compiling information about one topic like, "15 Signs You Are from Colorado" or "21 Sort of Healthy Ways to Enjoy Chocolate." The differences are listicles are usually found online; they comprise a few sentences about each point and a photo or GIF.

Personal Essay

Told in first person, these personal narratives are another great way to break into a publication. These pieces share a unique personal experience or moment with the readers. They can be funny, heartwarming, informative, inspirational, or poignant. Although they are based on your personal story, they need to revolve around a universal theme readers can relate to such as hope, fear, love, guilt … some overarching subject that allows the reader to connect with your story. (More information on writing and selling personal essays can be found in chapter nine.)

How-To

How-to articles present step-by-step sequential directions. Recipes, crafts, and DIY (do-it-yourself) projects are all examples of how-to's. These are typically straightforward without a lot of added narrative. In the introduction to this book I mention the handprint wreath craft idea I published in *Better Homes and Gardens*. This is an example of a how-to. Along with the text, I sent an example of the finished product.

Profile

This article features an interview with someone and is written in a narrative style with quotes from the subject woven throughout. The focus of the piece is usually on one aspect of the person's life or a specific accomplishment. The writer's goal for this type of piece is to ask good questions and dig deeper to provide a well-rounded view of the subject. I wrote a profile recently about the pianist George Winston. The focus was on his music, so I asked him questions about when he started playing the piano, his process for composing his pieces, musicians who influenced him, and what continues to keep him motivated after doing this for a few decades. I wove the answers to his questions throughout the article to give the reader a snapshot of George Winston and his music.

Review

A review provides the writer's evaluation on a product, a movie, a play, a book. It is an opinion, but it is more than just saying you liked or didn't like something. A good reviewer objectively examines the product and supports their views with examples and explanations. Knowing ahead of time the areas you will focus on is important. For instance, if you are reviewing the durability of a toy for young children, you aren't going to pay so much attention to how it looks.

You are going to see how it lasts after a toddler drags it around the house, drops it down the stairs, or steps on it. Make sure you focus your review on the product itself rather than your experience. If you are reviewing a movie and halfway through there are technical difficulties that create a ten-minute interruption, this should not impact your review. It may have been frustrating, but it's not fair to the movie's creator to let it affect the review. If you are writing a book review and the app you are using to read the digital book creates some hang-ups in the formatting and user experience, this has nothing to do with the quality of the story, plot, and characters and should not appear in the review.

Travel

For many, travel writing seems glamorous. But, as with any article, it takes work; it's more than jet-setting around the world to exotic locations. Visiting a destination when you have an assignment creates a different mindset than if you are there for vacation. You will be taking more notes, collecting information, and seeking experiences that fit with the readership of the publication. Travel pieces can take many different angles. You can do a historical walking tour, a weekend getaway, the best family-friendly activities in a city/state, or focus on a national park; the possibilities are almost endless.

Any time I travel I am always on the lookout for activities, locations, or events that would make good articles. I take photos, jot down notes, and collect information that may come in handy later. On many occasions I have come up with a travel idea once I got home and thought about it more. I am then grateful for the material I gathered during the trip.

Q&A (Question and Answer)

These have a simple format. The interviewer asks the question and the subject answers. This becomes the main part of the article. There is usually a short narrative introduction about the person being interviewed, but the rest is the questions and answers, verbatim. The key to writing a successful Q&A is to have thoughtful questions to ask the subject. Simple yes and no questions are not going to provide much information and won't be interesting to the reader. Well-crafted open-ended questions encourage a subject to reveal fascinating aspects about herself and her life.

Feature

Features are the mainstays of magazines. They are the longer articles found in the middle of each issue and the ones highlighted on the covers. Because of their length and the work involved in writing them, features pay more than the departments. These can be harder for new writers to break into because editors are committing a big portion of the magazine for that feature. If a writer doesn't follow through, the editor is left with a big empty space that needs to be filled. They're taking a risk with a writer without a track record, but it doesn't mean it is impossible to land a feature as a new writer.

One of my favorite features I worked on was "All Aboard to the Inside Passage" for *Family Motor Coaching* magazine. It allowed me to delve deeper into research about Alaska, a part of the country I love, and learn about the ferry system, which I find fascinating. I then had to be creative and write it up in a new and fresh way. The published feature covered eight pages in the middle of the issue and explored traveling on the Alaska Marine Highway to visit unique areas of the Inside Passage. I shared about the ferry system used to transport passengers to the small islands and coastal communities and how it worked. Then I wrote about five different towns along the route and gave the high points of each. The piece provided readers with interesting information about the ferry system and the towns, enabling them to decide if it was a trip they wanted to try or just enjoy reading about.

Back of Book (BOB)

The last page of a magazine is a single page and not a full two-page spread. Many publications have something special on that final page that is often more light and fun. It varies from magazine to magazine. *Mother Earth Living* has a photo and poem or quote, and *The Costco Connection* highlights two members on their back page. *AFAR* magazine has a short travel piece called "Just Back From." It is written in first person, includes a large full-page photo and gives a snapshot of a destination including a few places to visit. Check a few issues to see if this section is written by the same person or if it varies. If it's a different person each time, it's probably open to free-lance writers.

KNOW THE WRITER'S GUIDELINES

Writer's guidelines are the key to getting your articles into magazines. They spell out exactly what you need to do to submit your work, what types of articles they publish, length of pieces, pay rate, and other helpful details. Read the guidelines carefully and follow them when submitting your query or article. Becoming proficient at reading and understanding these guidelines will save you time and hassle in the long run because you will target the correct publications and make sure the right people see your submissions in the forms they want them in.

Where to Find the Guidelines

There are different options for finding writer's guidelines. Regardless of where you find the information, it is important to always seek out and understand what a magazine is looking for regarding submissions.

Market Guide Books (*Writer's Market*)

Writer's Market is the perfect resource for anyone looking to submit to a magazine and the best one in the industry to help you find markets. It contains hundreds of pages of information for consumer and trade publications, compiled into one book. Although it doesn't include every magazine on the market, it highlights many of them.

Each entry includes contact information, percent of freelance-written articles, a little about the magazine, types of articles they are looking for, word count, the pay rate, and tips for writers. When you find publications you are interested in pitching to, you can go to those magazines' websites for the most current information.

Online

Many sites online have put together lists of guidelines and links to various publications. Many times they are sorted by topics, making your search time more efficient. There is a list of these sites in the resource section in the back of the book.

Magazine Website

Most magazines have guidelines online for writers, sharing what they want you to send. Some publications have detailed guidelines that include:

- types of articles they are looking for
- which departments are open to freelancers
- what they want to see in a query letter
- how to send it to them
- tips for getting an assignment

Others have basic information with a general overview of what they are looking for and where to send the pitch. The submission guidelines are usually found in the About Us or Contact Us section on a magazine's website, which can sometimes be at the bottom of the page.

Ezines

There are ezines (electronic magazines) you can subscribe to that have market information that is e-mailed to you. Subscribing to these is a great way to learn about new markets. Here are a few of the more popular ones:

- FundsforWriters: www.fundsforwriters.com
- Freelance Writing: www.freelancewriting.com
- WritersWeekly.com: www.writersweekly.com

Understanding the Guidelines

Once you know where to find the guidelines, it is important you understand how to read them. Like I mentioned earlier, *Writer's Market* is a prime resource for many writers. General items to always pay attention to when you study these markets are the focus of the publication, lead time, topics covered, percentage of magazine written by freelance writers, rights, and payment.

The book includes a legend in the front section that explains the meanings of some of the symbols you see. Let's look at a couple of entries and decipher the different parts to better understand what the publication is looking for.

[1]$$$ DRAFT

[2]300 W. Clarendon Ave., Suite 155, Phoenix, AZ 85013. **E-mail:** editorial@draftmag.com. **Website:** www.draftmag.com. [3]**60% freelance written.** [4]Bimonthly magazine covering beer and men's lifestyle (including food, travel, sports, and leisure). [5]*"DRAFT* is

a national men's magazine devoted to beer, breweries, and the life-style and culture that surrounds it. Read by nearly 300,000 men aged 21-45, *DRAFT* offers formal beer reviews, plus coverage of food, travel, sports, and leisure. Writers need not have formal beer knowledge (though that's a plus!), but they should be experienced journalists who can appreciate beer and beer culture." [6]Estab. 2006. Circ. 275,000. [7]Byline given. [8]Pays on publication. [9] Offers 20% kill fee. [10]Publishes ms an average of 2 months after acceptance. [11]Editorial lead time 4 months. Submit seasonal material 6 months in advance. Accepts queries by e-mail. [12]Accepts simultaneous submissions. [13]Responds in 1 month to queries. Sample copy: $3 (magazine can also be found on most newsstands for $4.99). [14]Guidelines available at draftmag.com/submissions.

[15]**NONFICTION** [16]Do not want unsolicited mss, beer reviews, brewery profiles. [17]**Buys 80 mss/year.** [18]Query with published clips. [19]Length: 250-2,500 words. [20]**Pays 50-90¢ for assigned articles.** [21]Expenses limit agreed upon in advance.

1. The dollar signs before the magazine name give you an idea of the pay rate. The scale is zero to four dollar signs. If you are a newer writer, you might have better luck targeting lower-paying markets to start.

2. Every entry in *Writer's Market* starts with basic contact information and website.

3. This is the amount of the magazine written by freelance writers. For *Draft*, this number is sixty percent. That is a good amount and lets you know you have a good chance with a well-written, targeted pitch.

4. As you can see this publication is bimonthly, so it comes out every two months.

5. Then it explains the type of articles they seek and their target demographic: men ages 21-45. As you can see, this is more than a

magazine about beer; it is about the lifestyle that includes beer, but also food, travel, sports, and leisure. This is great to know because most people would not think to pitch a travel or sports idea to a beer magazine. They also provide a tip that writers don't have to know a lot about beer, but need to appreciate it.

6. We see that the magazine was established in 2006 and has a circulation of 275,000.

7. When it states a byline is given, it means your name will be on the article; typically, a one-sentence bio is also included at the end.

8. They pay on publication, which means you get your money after the article is available on the newsstands.

9. A kill fee is what you get paid if the article doesn't end up being published, yet you fulfilled your end of the contract with your submission. So if you were originally going to get three-hundred dollars for the article, *Draft* will pay you twenty percent, or sixty dollars.

10. Your article will be published about two months after it is accepted.

11. The lead time for this publication is four months. This means they are working four months ahead. If it is January, *Draft* is probably working on the May issue.

12. Simultaneous submissions (sending the same query or article to different publications) is fine with this magazine.

13. They will respond in one month to your query.

14. They have more guidelines on their website.

15. They take only nonfiction and don't want unsolicited articles (which means query first).

16. They spell out some article topics they don't want to see: beer reviews and brewery profiles.

17. They buy eighty manuscripts (articles) each year.

18. Send queries and not full articles. Also include your published clips. A clip is a copy of the published article as it appeared in the magazine or on the website, not the text you submitted for the piece. The best way to highlight clips is with a link to your website or to the magazine's website if the article is found there. Include queries in the body of the e-mail and not as an attachment. With so many potential computer viruses out there, many editors will not open attachments from people they don't know.

19. The length of the articles in this publication ranges from 250–2,500 words.

20. The pay rate is fifty to ninety cents per word.

21. They sometimes pay the expenses of a writer on assignment.

[1]$$$$ NATIONAL GEOGRAPHIC KIDS

[2]National Geographic Society, 1145 17th St. NW, Washington, DC 20036. **E-mail:** ashaw@ngs.org. [3]E-mail: chughes@ngs .org; asilen@ngs.org; kboatner@ngs.org. **Website:** www.kids. nationalgeographic.com. **Contact:** Catherine Hughes, science editor; Andrea Silen, associate editor; Kay Boatner, associate editor; Jay Sumner, photo director. [4]**70% freelance written**. Magazine published 10 times/year. [5]"It's our mission to find fresh ways to entertain children while educating and exciting them about their world." [6]Estab. 1975. Circ. 1.3 million. [7]Byline given. [8]Pays on acceptance. [9]Offers 10% kill fee. [10]Publishes ms an average of 6 months after acceptance. [11]Editorial lead time 6+ months. Submit seasonal material 6+ months in advance. [12]Accepts queries by mail. [13]Accepts simultaneous submissions. Sample copy for #10 SASE. Guidelines online.

[14]**NONFICTION** Needs general interest, humor, interview, technical. Query with published clips and résumé. Length: 100-1,000 words. [15]**Pays $1/word for assigned articles.**

[16]**COLUMNS** Freelance columns: Amazing Animals (animal heroes, stories about animal rescues, interesting/funny animal tales), 100 words; Inside Scoop (fun, kid-friendly news items), 50-70 words. Query with published clips. **Pays $1/word.**

Let's look at a children's market, *National Geographic Kids*.

1. This is a higher paying market with four dollar signs.

2. It gives contact information.

3. This entry gives the names of three different editors. Be sure to check the website to confirm these are still the correct editors.

4. It is seventy percent freelance written and comes out ten times per year.

5. They provide a general idea of the purpose of the magazine. Your queries should fall in line with this statement.

6. This publication has been around since 1975 and has a circulation of 1.3 million.

7. They give the writer a byline.

8. They pay on acceptance. This means once the final article has been turned into the editor and it is accepted, you will be paid. You will get your money before the magazine comes out.

9. The kill fee is ten percent.

10. The article is usually published about six months after acceptance.

11. They have a lead time of more than six months, so if you have an idea for a summer-related topic that fits for a June issue, you need to query in November.

12. It says they accept queries by mail, but a quick visit to their online guidelines shows they also accept queries by e-mail.

13. Simultaneous submissions (sending the same query or article to different publications) is fine with this magazine.

14. They explain the types of articles published and ask that you query with published clips (copies of the published article as it appeared in the magazine).
15. Pay rate is one dollar per word.
16. This magazine also has specific columns that are open to freelance writers. They give the word count for these departments and the pay rate of one dollar per word.

Article Example: Opinion Piece

TO GET PAID OR NOT GET PAID, THAT IS THE QUESTION

Since I began writing for magazines more than eighteen years ago, there is this notion out there that when you first start out, you need to write for free. That you should find small, local publications that will take your work but aren't going to pay you anything. This way, you'll have some publishing credits under your belt when you approach magazines that do pay their writers.

I don't believe this to be true at all. You are providing content and filling a need for the publications you submit to. You deserve to get paid. As with any job, the more experience you have, the more you should expect to earn. If you are fairly new to writing and don't have any publication credits or a degree in journalism, you shouldn't expect to start out getting thousands for your articles. That's not realistic. But I believe you should get paid something.

The first piece I ever published appeared in *Better Homes and Gardens*. It was a craft idea (with about 150 words of text). I received a couple hundred dollars for the idea, the text, and a sample of the craft. It's important to understand though, I did my due diligence. I researched the market, I understood the readership of this publication, and I understood their lead time. That increased my chances to have this idea published.

If you want to get paid for your magazine writing (and why wouldn't you?), then you need to take the same approach. You need to do your homework and study the markets you want to pitch. Do what you can to make an editor's job easier by giving her something she can use.

Are there times you should write for free? Yes—but not because you are just starting out. If you are looking to build a platform, a brand, or position yourself as an expert in a particular field, then you might consider writing articles for free. I have a friend who is a professional speaker. Her target audience is nurses and other health-care professionals. She wants to be seen as an expert in this area. She writes articles for nursing and health-care magazines and offers them for free as long as her bio (which includes her website and contact info) is included at the bottom of the article. Although she doesn't get paid, the return on her time investment is huge when potential clients read her articles, see her as an expert in the field, and hire her to give a keynote address.

With this being the one exception, I am here to say, you do not need to write for free. In addition, when you write for free, it lowers the bar for other writers. You help perpetuate the idea that we should write for free because it's good exposure for us. Exposure doesn't pay the bills; it doesn't even pay for a cup of coffee. Respect yourself as a writer and a professional, and seek out the writing opportunities that will pay you for your time and knowledge.

KNOW WHAT ARTICLES HAVE RECENTLY BEEN PUBLISHED

Once you know the reader, the styles, the types of articles, and the guidelines, you need to research issues from at least one year back to see if the potential ideas you are thinking of pitching, were recently covered.

When I study a new magazine, I will look it up online and when possible, I will print off the table of contents from the past six to twelve issues. Then I get a clear picture of the topics addressed over the past twelve months.

Tyler Moss with *Writer's Digest* magazine sees pitching a story that's the same or incredibly similar in subject matter to an article they recently published as the number one mistake writers make. "To an editor, this shows you haven't done your research, either reading recent issues of the magazine or by conducting a simple search on their website. It comes off as lazy and arrogant. Editors respect when a writer can demonstrate intimate knowledge of a publication, in which they come off as a sincere fan of the magazine and not just a salesperson trying to cut a deal."

Studying a magazine and understanding all you can about it will put you way ahead of others trying to break into this world. Editors will appreciate the time and energy you put in to knowing their readership and will reward you with assignments.

MAGAZINE RESEARCH CHECKLIST

____ Do you have a clear understanding about who reads the publication?

____ Do you understand the style and tone of the articles? Conversational? Informational?

____ Did you notice how often expert quotes are used?

____ Do you know what topics the magazine has covered in the last twelve months?

____ Do you know what types of articles they use?

____ Did you find the masthead and take note of the editors and contributing writers?

BIGGEST MISTAKE FROM NEW WRITERS

TOD JONES, MANAGING EDITOR FOR *THE COSTCO CONNECTION*: Not understanding that there needs to be a *connection* to Costco. The connection can be as simple as a profile of a Costco member or Costco supplier, or a topic that ties into a Costco product or service. Also pitching ideas for articles that we have recently done (not doing their homework).

JONAH OGLES, ARTICLES EDITOR FOR *OUTSIDE*: They don't report pitches. I totally understand that it's tough to report when you've yet to make money on a story. But the best pitches are the ones that read as if the writer has done half the work, and all I have to do is say, "OK, go out and finish the job." Just as important as reporting the pitch: It should read as if it's reported. That means including scene, setting, and quotes. The best pitches read like the first section of a story.

KATHERINE LAGRAVE, SENIOR DIGITAL EDITOR FOR *CONDÉ NAST TRAVELER*: Not having a time hook. I'll often get a blurb on something that sounds interesting, but doesn't answer the "Why are we covering this now?" question. To me, that's just an idea and not a pitch. With travel, I also tend to get a lot of "I'm going to [insert place]. Do you want anything?" queries from new writers. We typically never assign this way, and if we do, it's to writers we count as regular contributors.

KASEY CORDELL, FEATURES EDITOR FOR *5280*: A lack of understanding either of my publication, our timeline, or what makes something newsworthy.

TYLER MOSS, EDITOR-IN-CHIEF FOR *WRITER'S DIGEST MAGAZINE*: We're pretty consistent with the types of articles we feature, particularly in the Inkwell (the front-of-book department where most new writers break in). I'll receive queries on topics that are only tangentially related to writing or cover very general topics that lack a unique hook (for example, something like *10 Tips for Self-Publishing Your Book*). The best pitches are specific in subject and either explore something old in a fresh way or reveal something new and essential. You want your story to be an ideal amalgamation: an idea that's a perfect fit, but that the editor has never thought of.

MICHELLE THEALL, FORMER SENIOR EDITOR FOR *ALASKA* MAGA-ZINE: Going too big. Study the front of the book sections and submit a query for one of those short pieces, like a book review or a quick hit. We need that copy, and once you've nailed a short assignment, I know I can trust you to deliver something longer.

ROBBIN GOULD, EDITOR OF *FAMILY MOTOR COACHING*: Submitting queries that aren't relevant. My magazine is published by an association whose members own motor homes—motorized recreation vehicles. We focus on motor homes and the RV life-style enjoyed in them. We do not accept articles that describe the specific characteristics and use of towable RVs, such as travel trailers and fifth-wheels. Researching our publication can reveal our emphasis on motor homes.

Submitting incomplete queries. Please don't send the all-too-brief "Would you like to see an article about (TOPIC)?" with no further explanation. Unless that topic sounds particularly intriguing, an editor is likely to decline right away rather than request additional information.

MAKE A PLAN

Article Example: How To

CREATE A PITCH CALENDAR

Now that you have your ideas and have studied magazines and guidelines, it is time to put together a plan of action. You will want to create one that keeps you focused, minimizes feelings of overwhelm, and helps you organize your thoughts as well as your time.

A pitch calendar can help you do all that. It allows you to organize your ideas, the publications, and the time frame. It becomes a great visual to keep you moving forward and not get stuck when rejections come your way because they will. You may feel you are too busy to put together a pitch calendar, but the reality is, you are too busy not to make one. It will help you streamline the process and allow you to get more accomplished.

There are two ways you can organize your calendar. One can be focused on specific publications and one can be focused on the ideas.

PUBLICATION PITCH CALENDAR

The goal of this calendar is to focus your time and energy on the publications you want to pitch. Because it takes time to study different magazines, this approach allows you to become an expert on a few, then create your ideas based on these publications. You will become familiar with the style, the length of articles, and the types of articles they have covered. You will learn the magazine inside and out, and the editors will appreciate that. It may take time to break in, but persistence is key.

STEPS

1. Pick three to five magazines you want to study.

2. Write the names of those magazines across the top of the chart.

3. On the far left column, write the months, one in each box. Start with the month you plan to start sending out queries.

4. For each publication create a list of all the ideas you can think of that are a good fit.

5. Look at your list of ideas and fill in the boxes for the publication and the best month to send off the query. You will probably have more ideas than spaces on the chart. Hold on to those for a later time. Keep in mind the lead time for the publications you have chosen. With some ideas it doesn't matter when you pitch them; with others that are seasonal, you need to think about four to six months in advance, or whatever time frame is listed in the writer's guidelines. A query for an article about summer travel should be sent out in January; a back-to-school pitch should go out in March; plan on sending Christmas ideas in early summer.

PUBLICATION MONTH	SUNSET (LIFESTYLES)	FAMILY MOTOR COACHING (RECREATIONAL VEHICLE LIFE-STYLE)	HIGHLIGHTS (CHILDREN'S)	ENTREPRENEUR (BUSINESS)
JANUARY	A Visit to Colorado Wineries	Profile of an Avid RV Family	History of Ice Cream	Impress Anyone in 2 Seconds
FEBRUARY	10 Tips to Host the Perfect Outdoor Party	Get the Most out of Your RV Storage	How Whales Communicate	5 Effective Social Media Strategies
MARCH	Hidden Gems of Portland	Fall Foliage Must-Sees	Instruments Made from Gourds (Seasonal-fall)	Profile of the CEO of a Successful Startup
APRIL	5 Unique Fall Festivals in the West	Tips for Traveling with Pets	Holidays Around the World	How to Make Crowdfunding Work for You

IDEA PITCH CALENDAR

This approach focuses on different ideas and slants to fit certain types of magazines. You will become well versed on your topics and be able to create effective ways to tailor those ideas.

1. Choose three to five types of magazines: food and drink, regional, science, sports. … If you are using *Writer's Market* as your source for guidelines, use the categories found in the Consumer Magazines and Trade Journals sections. This will make it easier when you research specific markets for each idea.

2. Look over all the ideas you have collected. Choose the ones that fit each magazine category, and put them in the appropriate squares during the month you want to write and send out the query.

3. Research specific magazines and add those names below each idea.

4. For each month write the queries you have in the boxes and send them off.

5. If a query comes back with a *no thank you*, find another publication; tailor the query to that magazine and send it out.

TYPE OF PUBLICATION MONTH	WOMEN'S IDEA	TRAVEL	CHILDREN'S	OUTDOORS
JANUARY	Personal Essay: My Nest is now Empty. Am I Supposed to be Sad? **Magazine:** *Woman's Day*	10 Must-Visit Camping Destinations This Summer **Magazine:** *Budget Travel*	History of Ice Cream **Magazine:** *Highlights*	Profile of a Young Rock Climber **Magazine:** *Outside*
FEBRUARY	Pet Etiquette 101 **Magazine:** *Real Simple*	Country Hotels in Spain **Magazine:** *Condé Nast Traveler*	Identify and Deal with Dangerous Bugs **Magazine:** *Boys' Life*	5 Tips for Stress-Free Camping with Young Children **Magazine:** *Family Motor Coaching*
MARCH	What if Your Kid is the Bully? **Magazine:** *Working Mother*	Family-Friendly San Francisco **Magazine:** *National Geographic Traveler*	Profile of a Teenage Girl Impacting her Community **Magazine:** *New Moon Girls*	Get in Shape for Hiking **Magazine:** *Backpacker*

CHAPTER FOUR

• • •

WRITING AN EFFECTIVE QUERY LETTER

Once you have done your upfront research and have found a magazine that is a good fit for your idea, it is time to reach out to an editor with an intriguing query letter. I know I am in the minority when I say this, but I love writing query letters. There is something appealing about coming up with the idea, finding the perfect market, doing the initial research, then weaving it all together into a great pitch that lands me an assignment. Once you understand how to compose an effective query, hopefully you too will find joy in the process. Each query is going to be different and personalized for the individual publication, but there are common elements to keep in mind with each one you write.

Knowing how to compose a great query is the cornerstone of your magazine writing life. First and foremost, editors are busy people (see sidebar on the next page). They are working on many different aspects of the magazine. Reading your query letter is a small part of their week, so it has to grab their attention quickly. This one-page sales pitch is your chance to not only sell your idea but show the editor you are a competent writer, you have a good understanding of the topic you are pitching, and you understand the magazine's readership. The letter should be professional and written in a style and tone similar to the article you want to write.

Kasey Cordell, editor with *5280*, spends less than five minutes reading a query. "I like to see: a clear (and well-written) articulation of what the story is, why it's a story for our readers, why it's a story for our readers *now* (news peg), an indication you've already done some reporting, what section the story fits in, and how long you're expecting it will be or what shape you imagine it will take (narrative, roundup, infographic, etc.)."

Tod Jones, editor with *The Costco Connection*, likes short, clear pitches and wants to be able to efficiently organize them. "I don't like to receive several different themed pitches in an e-mail, as it makes pitches I want to keep for consideration more difficult to file in an appropriate month or topic folder."

Jonah Ogles with *Outside* wants writers to treat the pitch in the query letter like a story. "It should be clear that they've done reporting, that they know how to craft a scene (including quotes), and that they're thinking smartly about structure and organization. If those things are there, I try to develop a relationship with the writer, even if that idea isn't quite right for the magazine."

TYPICAL WORKDAY/WEEK FOR A MAGAZINE EDITOR

THESE EDITORS GIVE A SMALL PEEK INTO THEIR WORLD

TOD JONES, EDITOR FOR *THE COSTCO CONNECTION*: I work 5:30 A.M. to 3, Monday through Friday. Overseeing current issue, mapping and organizing future issues, editing submissions, reading through queries, making assignments for in-house staff or freelancers, attending staff/production meetings, writing up in-house pieces (occasionally), authorizing freelance payments.

JONAH OGLES, EDITOR FOR *OUTSIDE*: I split time between our print magazine (where I edit six to nine features or packages a year) and our site. I start my day with our news meeting, where editors gather to talk about the news of the day and what stories *Outside* should be covering on the site. Then I top-edit and do a QC/final read of stories for the site until lunch. In the afternoon,

I try to actually edit: I read stories. I draft memos. I call writers and talk through changes. Then each afternoon one of our sections/channels meets to discuss story ideas for our various coverage areas: fitness, gear, travel, etc. The one thing I don't do daily is read pitches—which unfortunately only happens on Fridays (or every other Friday, when I'm especially busy). There's a lot of other stuff squeezed in there (coffee, mostly), but when I'm firing on all cylinders, that's what I'm up to.

KATHERINE LAGRAVE, EDITOR FOR *CONDÉ NAST TRAVELER*: My days are pretty much the same throughout the week. In the morning, I come in and answer some e-mails before I help get trending content out the door. After lunch, I spend time working on other content we plan to publish that day—features, galleries—and look at the week ahead to turn around edits on stories. I try to carve out some time each day to set aside pitches too; otherwise they can easily get lost in my in-box. One day a week, I take a look at these pitches and assign, respond with questions, or pass along to other editors.

KASEY CORDELL, EDITOR FOR *5280*: It depends entirely on what part of the production cycle we're in, as well as what I'm working on that day. Suffice it to say, my workdays over the course of a month are filled with reporting, writing, editing, concepting, revising, planning meetings, collaborating with my art team, meeting with freelancers and sources, reading and revising proofs, interacting with fact checkers, fulfilling requests from our marketing department (such as radio and television appearances), representing the magazine at events around the city, answering e-mail (that should probably be number one) including pitches from writers. That's a start.

TYLER MOSS, (FORMER MANAGING EDITOR) EDITOR-IN-CHIEF FOR *WRITER'S DIGEST*: As managing editor, my typical week is a balance of shepherding through the editorial process whatever issue we're working on and looking ahead to future issues. The former means reading and rereading articles in different iterations as they are first turned in, then revised, then designed on the page and so on. The latter means looking at article pitches and acquiring new work or considering bigger-picture items like issue themes, WD interview subjects, or potential new columns.

MICHELLE THEALL, FORMER SENIOR EDITOR FOR *ALASKA*: I put all queries into a file on my server and review them once a week. The rest of the time, I'm editing, writing, and assigning out. Depending on where we are in the production cycle, I'll also be proofing layouts and copyediting before signing off on an issue.

ROBBIN GOULD, EDITOR FOR *FAMILY MOTOR COACHING*: Obviously, magazine work is ruled by deadlines. After an issue is "put to bed," our planning for future issues begins or resumes. It's also time to attend to other details. I have a week or so to catch up on e-mails, review manuscripts and queries, send article offers, request check payments, assign editorial projects, etc. And because I work for an association publication, I have numerous other responsibilities within the organization also. As the month progresses, work on the upcoming issue intensifies—"dummying," or scheduling material for that issue; editing and proofreading copy; writing captions; reviewing layouts; checking final page proofs; reviewing the digital issue. Every day is different, yet the overall process is a cycle.

Before diving deep into this topic, here is a quick overview of the different components of an effective query letter:

- Salutation
- Hook
- Article Content
- Specifics
- Purpose
- Qualifications
- Call to Action
- Closing

As you understand the essential parts of query letters, they will become easier to write. You will learn how much research you need to do to understand your topic, and you will come up with your own system for creating an effective pitch.

Let's look at each separate component and what each should include.

COMPONENTS OF A QUERY LETTER

Salutation (Dear Mr. Smith)

Names are important; they are what identify us. Everyone likes to be personally addressed, and editors are no different. It is going to take a little work, but find the correct editor to direct your query to. This may seem insignificant since it has nothing to do with the idea you are pitching, but I can't stress enough the importance of this small detail.

Tyler Moss, editor-in-chief for *Writer's Digest* magazine, solidifies the point: "If the letter is addressed to an editor who hasn't been at *Writer's Digest* for years, or has a greeting like 'Dear Sir or Madam,' I'm likely to reject it right away."

As I have mentioned, if you are using *Writer's Market* don't assume the contact information is the most up-to-date. For the most current information, go to the magazine's website. Many times it will have a list of staff. Another way to get this information is to look at the most recent issue of publication and read the masthead. This is the list of staff found within the first few pages of the magazine. It is typically a long, thin list that takes up about a third of the page. See if you can find the name of a managing editor. If you can't find a name, then make a quick phone call to the publishing company. Ask for the editorial department and say something like, "Whom should I direct a travel query to?" Find out the correct spelling and the editor's e-mail. Always find a specific editor's name even when the writer's guidelines say to send queries to a generic e-mail address such as editor@magazine.com.

Unless you know the editor, use a formal salutation: Mr., Mrs., or Ms. This shows the editor you are serious about your writing and you understand this is a business transaction. If you are not sure if the editor is a man or woman, put their full name. Once you have established initial communication, take note of the name they use to close their correspondences with you and use that name if it is different than your initial salutation.

Hook

To catch fish, you need to use flies and bait that are going to attract their attention. Otherwise you will be wasting your time. Writing a good query is similar. You need a good hook that will lure the editor within the first one to three sentences and encourage her to keep reading and ultimately assign you the article. Without that intriguing opening, the editor will move on to the next query.

Tyler Moss says, "If a pitch is concise and compelling with a solid hook, and the writer has trustworthy credentials and/or an irresistible voice, I'm sure to follow up."

"I typically get the first sentence or two, and if you've hooked me there, I'll read on," says Michelle Theall. "The writing should be similar to the story you plan to tell, except more concise. Definitely put a link to your website so I can view clips."

A good lede can make the difference between a *yes* and a *no thank you*. So what makes a good lede? A good lede is one that piques interest, elicits questions, and compels the editor to want to continue reading. There are different ways you can create a good lede.

Anecdote

An interesting anecdote is a great way to draw in the reader, in this case the editor. We all like a good story because stories connect us. They give us a way to relate to someone else.

> **EXAMPLE:** Every winter, Denise—a 45-year-old schoolteacher from western New York—could predict the regular onslaught of cold-induced asthma attacks and an annual sinus infection. But this past winter, she remained healthy all season—a first for her. [Latona, V. (2015, Jul/Aug). Eat Your Way Healthy. *Mother Earth Living,* 46]

Statistic

A good statistic is intriguing and will urge the editor to read more to find out how it relates to what you are pitching.

> **EXAMPLE:** According to the National Soap and Detergent Association, getting rid of clutter would eliminate forty percent of housework in the average home.

Question

Opening a query letter or an article with a question can be tricky. The goal is to ask a question that elicits the response you are looking for. For instance, if you ask, "Have you ever wondered what it's like to live in a small mountain town?" and the editor says to himself, "no," he probably won't read any further. Instead, create a question that is more open ended or one that only has one good answer.

> **EXAMPLE:** What is your life's true purpose? Many of us on the path to self-improvement and greater happiness have pondered this question. But have you ever sat down, in the quiet, and waited for an answer? [Johnson, H.R. (2016, June). Mindful Moments, Unlocking Your True Potential, *Live Happy,* 16]

Humor

If you are pitching a humorous article, you need to grab the editor with a funny opening that sets the tone for the rest of the query and for the article you want to write.

> **EXAMPLE:** It begins with shaky hands, then it's followed by shortness of breath, and it finally ends with the realization that you've spent your gambling allotment for the day. Now what?

Quote

Do you have an interesting quote from someone you interviewed for your query? If so, consider opening your pitch with the quote. This is especially true if you are pitching a profile.

> **EXAMPLE:** "There seems to be this myth in publishing that spills over into the indie world, that you write one book, you make a million dollars and your life is changed."

Scene Setting

Some publications have more visual imagery than others. If you are pitching to one of these magazines, then it is a good idea to open your query by setting the scene. Paint a picture and put the reader there.

> **EXAMPLE:** The rest of the world disappeared as I entered the lush, green forest in Ketchikan. A quiet stillness set in, yet I knew the verdant foliage surrounding me was very much alive. The rain tried to break through, but the dense canopy blocked much of it, keeping me fairly dry. Berry bushes and ferns helped create the deep, green forest floor, and a crystal-clear creek meandered through in search of the Pacific Ocean. This incredible accomplishment of nature is part of the world's largest rain forest in the Tongass National Forest in Alaska.

Here are some other examples of ledes.

Good Ledes:

- Most of the year, Nome is a hardworking community of 3,500 residents who fish and mine for gold from the wind-whipped outpost on the edge of the Bering Sea. But for a week each March when the Iditarod comes to town, this far-flung hub of commerce in northwest Alaska becomes "Mardi Gras on Ice." [Redal, W.R. (2014, March). Welcome to Nome, a.k.a. Mardi Gras on Ice, *Alaska*, 36]

I love this lede because it sets the scene by describing the Nome community, which aligns with what many of us think about a small Alaskan town. We also know what the Iditarod is, but then it flips all of that upside down when it says the town becomes Mardi Gras on Ice. Now I am intrigued. Alaska and New Orleans are two places I would never think of together.

- Few men are so successful in a chosen field that their name becomes synonymous with their profession. But racing legend Mario Andretti has achieved that iconic status. [Price, D. E. (2016, June). Living His Passion at Full Speed, *Live Happy*, 28]

This one is clear cut and gets right to the point—this is going to be about Andretti and how he achieved status and became a legend. Anyone with the slightest interest in him will want to read more.

- Silverpeak apothecary is the only cannabis shop in Aspen, and probably all of Colorado—perhaps the world—where a seventy-four-year-old, four-foot-eleven, bespectacled Jewish grandmother greets you at the door. [Bethea, Charles (2016, March). Haute Times, *Outside*, 62]

Similar to the Mardi Gras on Ice lede, this one combines two things that we don't normally associate. I want to know more about this cannabis shop where a small-statured senior citizen is greeting people at the door. Regardless of your stance on the legalization of marijuana, this is intriguing.

Weak Ledes

- Each year people come from all over to attend the Telluride Bluegrass Festival.
  - *This lede lends itself to asking "So what?" It needs more details and something unique about the festival.*
  - **STRONGER VERSION:** For four days every June, the twenty-four hundred residents of the small mountain town of Telluride prepare for the invasion of forty-eight thousand music lovers who trek in from all over the country to attend the annual Telluride Bluegrass Festival, now in its forty-fifth year.

- Every parent wants to better communicate with his or her teen.
  - *This feels like an obvious statement. Instead it would be better to open with an interesting statistic or with a solution to this dilemma.*
  - **STRONGER VERSION:** In a recent study by Harvard University, sixty-seven percent of all parents felt they had poor communication with their teens. Tina Smith claims she has a solution that will drop this number to zero.

- John Bates, a fourteen-year-old from Sacramento, California, has a special talent.
  - *This lede feels like it is trying to lead up to an important point. It is best to get to the point right away.*
  - **STRONGER VERSION:** John Bates, a fourteen-year-old from Sacramento, California, is the youngest computer programmer to ever work at Google.

Article Content

This is the bulk of your query. If the editor has read this far, he is interested in the initial idea, and this is where you have to sell it. You need to prove that you are an authority on the topic by explaining the main points you want to cover in the article. Also think about "Why now?" What makes this idea relevant at this point in time? Is there something going on in the news it is related to? Is there an important anniversary coming up? Is there an upcoming event tied to the topic, like Veterans Day or National Breast Cancer Awareness Month or Grandparents Day? Connecting it to something else it makes it more timely and hopefully more appealing to an editor. All of this information needs to be explained in about one paragraph.

The style of your query should match the tone and style you intend to use in the article, should you get the assignment. If you are pitching a humor piece and your query is dry and filled with boring statistics, you won't get the assignment. If, on the other hand, you get the editor laughing, then you have a better chance for a positive response.

This paragraph is also a good place to put any relevant research you may have at this point in the process. Did you find some interesting facts? Some great resources? It will show the editor you have a good understanding of the topic.

Here is an example from a query I sent to a writing magazine exploring the importance of social media in a writer's life. The query opened with a few lede sentences followed by current statistics of the impact of social media. Then I needed to explain the main components of the article with this information:

> I am proposing a feature article that explores this topic of "Does Social Media Really Work?" so writers can decide if it is something they should be spending their valuable writing time on. My plan is to talk to and interview agents, editors, publishers, readers, and published authors to answer the following questions regarding Twitter, Facebook, blogs, and LinkedIn:

- Does an effective social media presence have a direct correlation to increased book sales?
- Are readers of certain genres more influenced by social media? (I found that romance readers weren't; but what about other genres: YA, SF, Mystery, Nonfiction ...?)
- Why are agents and editors pushing so hard for a strong social media presence?
- Are there social media outlets that are more effective than others?

Specifics

This is the place to explain the specifics of the article: word count, a department if applicable, possible experts you are going to interview, and other information pertinent to the piece. To determine your estimated word count, refer to the writer's guidelines where the average word count for each department is usually spelled out. If not, look through the magazine to see the length of the different pieces. One page of article text is approximately five hundred words. Sharing the specifics gives the editor a clear picture of where the article will fit in the publication and shows her you did your homework. It makes her more confident that you read the magazine and have a good understanding of the readership.

This example is from a query I submitted to *The Costco Connection.* I wanted to highlight a church organization making a positive impact in their community:

> I am proposing an article that highlights this wonderful Costco member organization for your Member Profiles department or for a feature. For the article I will talk with the staff of Serve 6.8, the volunteers, and those who have been positively impacted by the organization, to get their insights and stories. In addition, I will provide a little history of Serve 6.8 and highlight some of the ways they have helped.

Purpose

In one sentence, share the purpose of your article. Will your article inform, educate, inspire, or entertain? By your stating this, the editor will understand what the readers will get from the article.

For instance, with the social media article for writers I included this to show the purpose of my article:

> My plan is to explore this topic from all angles, share with your readers what I find, and allow them to decide whether social media is good use of their time.

Qualifications (Why You?)

This is your place to shine and even brag about yourself a little. You need to convince the editor that you are the perfect person to write this article. This is where you need to highlight your experiences, your expertise, and any published articles you have.

If you do not have any published clips (previously published articles), don't mention it. Instead, expand more on your experiences that relate to your article. If you are pitching a parenting piece and you have six kids, mention that. It clearly positions you as someone with experience in the parenting field. If your degree relates to what you are pitching, share that. Membership in relevant associations or organizations can be included as well.

If you have published articles, then highlight a few of the most recent that closely relate to the type of piece you are pitching. There is no need to list every one. If you have a website where you have your clips or there are some online, include those links. If you don't have a website or links, then let the editor know you are happy to e-mail published clips on request.

Call to Action

You want to end the letter with a call to action for the editor, something that encourages her to contact you. Be assertive, but not pushy with "I know this is going to be a great article that you will definitely want" or too wimpy with "I haven't published anything before and my writing skills aren't great, but I really hope you will take a chance on me." Instead, it can be as simple as, "I look forward to talking with you more about this idea."

Closing

End the query with a closing of your choice: Sincerely, Thank you, Regards … then put your name, followed by your contact information.

Submitting

Most magazines accept and want queries by e-mail. Gone are the days of sending them through the mail. When sending a query via e-mail, include your query itself in the body of the e-mail unless directed otherwise in the guidelines. With so many potential computer viruses out there, many editors will not open attachments from writers they don't know. Once you get an assignment, it is okay to attach contracts and finished articles. The editor now knows you and trusts what you are sending.

When creating the e-mail, don't cut and paste directly from Microsoft Word. Sometimes there are special characters that show up for the recipient that you didn't know were there. To avoid this, you can do one of two things:

- Save the file as a plain text (.txt) file. You do this by clicking on File in your menu bar, then click on Save As. Below the file name, you can choose the type of file you want it to save as, in this case a .txt. This will create a new file in addition to the original word file. You can then copy and paste this text into the body of the e-mail.

- Copy the text and paste it into Notepad. Adjust any of the necessary formatting. Then copy the Notepad text and paste it into the body of the e-mail.

Stick to basic font choices in the serif classification like Times New Roman and Georgia. Avoid using fancy fonts. Editors prefer standard ones that are easier to read.

Once you have the query in the e-mail, put something in the subject line to catch the attention of the editor but also for search purposes later, when the editor is trying to find your query. I always put my name, query, and the title, for example, Flanagan QUERY: The Benefits of Chocolate and the Creative Process.

If the guidelines have you sending the e-mail to a generic e-mail address like editor@magazine.com, it is in your best interest to find a specific person to send it to; then in the subject line, put it to her attention: Attn. Jane Smith QUERY: The Benefits of Chocolate and the Creative Process_Flanagan. I always add my name at the end as well, to make it easy for an editor to search if they want to reference it in the future.

Do one final spell check before sending it off. Then record on a query tracking sheet (more about this in chapter eight) what you sent and to whom you sent it.

Query Follow-Up

I typically wait two weeks before I follow up with an editor with a quick e-mail. I will include the original text and query at the bottom, then say something like "I am following up to check on the status of the query, The Benefits of Chocolate on the Creative Process, I sent you on Aug. 9." I keep it short and sweet. In the subject line I put, "FOLLOW UP" and then the subject heading from the original e-mail.

Simultaneous Submissions

This is when you send the same query to different publications. As mentioned in chapter three in the Know the Writer's Guidelines section, some magazines find it acceptable to do this. Others don't. Personally I tailor my queries to a single publication, so I rarely send the same one out to different places at the same time.

Katherine LaGrave, editor with *Condé Nast Traveler,* understands it is easier to pitch a few editors at a time and not tailor it specifically to one magazine, but she notices when a writer has taken the time to customize the query. "If your pitch may not be right for me at the moment, I'll still notice the amount of work you put into it and will be more likely than not to respond to you and encourage you to pitch more."

If you are sending out simultaneous submissions, mention it at the end of the query. If one of the publications offers you an assignment, it is courteous to let the other editors know that you are withdrawing your submission.

Multiple Submissions

This is when you send multiple pitches to the same magazine editor in one e-mail. If nothing is mentioned in the guidelines, send a quick e-mail asking if the editor is okay with this. It may seem like a more efficient way to send your ideas, but it may make more work for the editor in the long run if they have a certain system for sorting queries.

EXCEPTIONS TO THE QUERY RULE

While most magazines want you to send a query first, there are some exceptions to this rule. With the following types of writing, instead of a query you will send a cover letter with the finished piece.

- FOB (Front of the Book)
- BOB (Back of the Book)
- Reprint
- Personal Essay
- Craft Idea
- Recipe
- Puzzles

COVER LETTER TEMPLATE:

Dear _____,

Enclosed below is (put the title or what you are including) for your consideration.

One sentence about the piece you are submitting.

If it fits within a certain department, mention that in another sentence.

One sentence bio if you feel it is necessary.

Sincerely,

Janet Smith

(include contact information here)

Include the piece here in the e-mail.

QUERY LETTER EXAMPLES

Here is a query from early in my freelance career. It follows the format I shared earlier and the one I have found works best for me. I use this most of the time, but there are instances when I change the order a bit—maybe put the "why me" first, if that is relevant at the beginning, or I add more details for a longer piece. Regardless of the specific order, the components of a query remain the same.

Dear Ms. Smith,

It begins with shaky hands, then it's followed by shortness of breath and it finally ends with the realization that you've spent your gambling allotment for the day. Now what?

I've heard people say there is more to do in Las Vegas than just gambling. The truth is, when I go, all I seem to do is try my luck at winning it big. Part of the reason is the slot machines and roulette tables actually call to me, and the other reason is I have never taken the time to find all the activities Vegas has to offer. I know there are shows to see and even a Hoover Dam tour, but I am certain there are many other things to do in this playground for adults.

I am proposing a light, roundup-style article, sharing with your readers, twenty fun, offbeat activities to try in Las Vegas when gambling just isn't hitting the jackpot anymore. Next month I will be visiting Vegas, and I plan to pull myself away from slot machines and personally investigate the wonders of Las Vegas. I will check out the hotels, virtual reality game rooms, swimming pools, and shopping areas. I will also conduct informal surveys at the blackjack table: "Excuse me, sir, what is your favorite roller coaster on the strip?" "Which water show at the Bellagio did you like the best?" With this information, your readers will never be at a loss of things to do when their luck is running dry.

I am a freelance writer from Colorado who occasionally likes to leave the clean mountain air behind and travel to bustling cities like Las Vegas. My work has appeared in various publications including the *Chicago Tribune, Woman's World, Colorado Homes & Lifestyles*, and *Better Homes and Gardens*.

Clips are available upon request. Photos are available for this article.

I look forward to hearing from you soon.

Sincerely,

Kerrie Flanagan

1234 Street Name
City, State, Zip
Phone
E-mail
Website

Below is the article that resulted from that query letter. (Since this is an older article, some of the information is outdated—in case you are visiting Vegas and hoped to see all these attractions.)

A few things to note with the article:

1. Notice the opening of the article is the same as the opening of my query. Typically, if I plan to open a query with an anecdote, I write one that will also work as the beginning of the article.

2. The tone of my query matches the tone of the article. Even though it is a roundup with lots of information, there is a still light humor woven throughout.

Article Example: Roundup

20 THINGS TO DO IN LAS VEGAS WHEN YOU DON'T WANT TO GAMBLE

It begins with shaky hands, then it's followed by shortness of breath and it finally ends with the realization that you've spent your gambling allotment for the day. Now what?

The first thing to do is leave the comfort and safety of the blackjack table or slot machine and venture outside. If you don't know how to get out, ask a cocktail waitress and she can direct you. Once outside, breathe in the hot, semi-fresh air and stroll down the strip. After getting acclimated to life on the "outside," begin planning your adventure, free of chips, cards and noisy slot machines. Consider:

1.) ROLLER COASTERS—Vegas has many unique coasters. Circus, Circus is home to the Canyon Blaster, the only indoor double-loop, double-corkscrew roller coaster. Speed: The Ride, located in the Sahara, takes passengers around a loop and up a 224-foot climb at speeds topping 70 mph and then retraces the same path in reverse.

2.) GOLF—Head to one of Las Vegas's 64 golf courses and tee up! Golf greats like Arnold Palmer and Jack Nicklaus designed some of these award-winning courses. If your mind is still on gambling, try the Legacy Golf Club where the tee boxes on the 10th hole are in the shape of spades, clubs, diamonds, and hearts.

3.) RED ROCK CANYON—To get farther off the strip, head to the Mojave Desert. Located about 30 minutes away, the Red Rock Canyon National Conservation Area is filled with beauty and wonders of nature. Travel the area on foot, horseback, or a bike. But don't forget your water!

4.) ART—See Picasso, van Gogh, Matisse, and many other world-renowned artists on display in the fine art galleries located on the strip. The Guggenheim Las Vegas and Guggenheim Hermitage Museum are located in The Venetian. The Bellagio hosts the Gallery of Fine Art and the Wynn Collections on the site of the former Desert Inn hotel.

5.) COMEDY—After losing money gambling, you may think there isn't much to laugh at, but Vegas has a variety of comedy clubs and big-name comedians. Rita Rudner is a regular at New York, New York. Smaller clubs hosting well-known and new comics can be found at Excalibur, Harrah's, and the Riviera.

6.) TRAM RIDES—Free, air-conditioned tram rides offer scenic views of the west side of the strip. Start at the south end of the strip at Mandalay Bay and go all the way to Treasure Island with short walks between trams.

7.) UNUSUAL SHOWS—Leave it to the entertainment capital of the world to offer some truly unique shows. The Blue Man Group combines drums, comedy, music, and color in a multimedia production unlike any other. Cirque du Soleil at the Bellagio, ventures into aquatic theater with "O," where a cast of 81 artists perform in, on, and above water.

8.) SPAS—For a relaxing escape, try one of Las Vegas's thirty spas. Swedish massage, reflexology, aromatherapy, saunas, whirlpools, pedicures, manicures, and herbal wraps are all available. *Condé Naste Traveler* voted the Canyon Ranch SpaClub at The Venetian one of the top ten spas in the United States.

9.) MUSEUMS—Las Vegas and flashy go hand in hand, and the museums are no exception. The Liberace museum and the Elvis-a-Rama Museum take a glimpse into the lives of these two flamboyant legends. Find flashy signs at The Neon Museum and flashy characters at the Casino Legends Hall of Fame.

10.) SHOPPING—Visit Venice, Paris, and Rome without ever leaving Las Vegas. Walk on quaint cobblestone streets, stroll by the Grand Canal, and view Roman statues at themed shopping venues at The Venetian, Paris, and Caesars Palace.

11.) FREE SHOWS—Believe it or not, every evening there are free shows in Las Vegas. Granted, they don't last long, and it's standing room only, but they're worth seeing. The Buccaneer Bay Pirate Battle, filled with action and pyrotechnics, happens in front of Treasure Island. A volcano's fiery eruption occurs in front of the Mirage every 15 minutes. The Fountains of Bellagio put on a spectacular show choreographed to music by artists such as Frank Sinatra, Elton John, and Luciano Pavarotti.

12.) WILDLIFE—Tigers, flamingos, dolphins, sharks … Las Vegas has it all. View the Dolphin Habitat, large cats, and an elephant at the Mirage. Find flamingos, penguins, and turtles at the Flamingo Resort. Enjoy an exotic bird show and tigers at the Tropicana. And journey through a replica of an ancient temple ruin and view the sharks at the Mandalay Bay Shark Reef.

13.) PEOPLE WATCHING—Watch the many interesting characters and enjoy a nice meal at Mon Ami Gabi located in the Paris Resort. It offers both patio seating where a cool mist sprays on the patio diners on hot summer days and a superb view of the strip.

14.) LASER SHOWS—On the hour in The Forum Shops at Caesars Palace, Roman statues come to life during a 7-minute special effects spectacular. In Downtown is the Fremont Street Experience covering four street blocks. Brilliantly colored images are choreographed to 540,000 watts of sound.

15.) THRILL RIDES—Looking for some excitement? The Big Shot at the Stratosphere shoots you 160 feet into the air with a force of 4Gs before you free-fall back to the launchpad. Another is the Inverter at Circus, Circus. This two-minute ride flips you 360 degrees at mind-blowing speeds.

16.) POOLS—Resort owners spared no expense when designing their pools. Mandalay Bay and the Monte Carlo have wave pools and lazy rivers. At the Flamingo, penguins and flamingos share the 15-acre pool area with swimmers. Beautiful waterfalls, fountains, and palms make this a perfect spot to unwind.

17.) 3-D RIDES—3-D motion simulator rides take you on a multisensory adventure that is out of this world. You move right into the action with the large screens and moving seats. See the Race for Atlantis at the Forum Shops and In Search of the Obelisk at the Luxor.

18.) TOURS—Who can resist chocolate? Just five miles off the strip is the Ethel M. Chocolate Factory, offering daily tours and samples. Next to MGM Grand is the four-story M&M's World, offering free tours and a lot of fun!

19.) FLOWERS—Crafted by a team of 100 horticulturalists, the Bellagio's conservatory features elegant, elaborate arrangements of about 7,500 plants and flowers in its bright, airy atrium.

20.) AND, if all else fails, dress up like Elvis and crash a convention.

MORE QUERY LETTER EXAMPLES

Here is a query letter from freelance writer Stacey McKenna that was sent to *STIR Journal*. She said, "It was one of my first paid publications and about something I was very excited to write." It resulted in the article "Displaced and Pushed out of Sight." (www.stirjournal .com/2015/12/09/displaced-and-pushed-out-of-sight)

Stacey does a great job with this query. She opens right away with some strong statistics regarding homelessness. The next few paragraphs go into more depth, explaining the problems surrounding this issue. She follows that with the specifics of what she is proposing and then her qualifications including links to published clips.

Hi Laurel,

In 2014, over 500,000 Americans were estimated homeless. Despite this national decline of 2.3%, homelessness rose in 17 states, including Colorado. As people struggle with unemployment and a shortage of affordable housing, the risk continues to grow.

Most places lack the resources to combat underlying causes or help those who are housing insecure. Yet the growing response nationwide has been to criminalize those without indoor shelter. According to the National Law Center on Homelessness & Poverty, 34% of U.S. cities ban public camping, 57% prohibit it in certain areas and 43% disallow sleeping in vehicles. Others have policies against sleeping in public, begging, and sharing food with homeless people.

No Right to Rest, a survey of homelessness throughout Colorado, found that most people without homes had had run-ins with law enforcement because of these "crimes of homelessness." Of 441 homeless individuals surveyed, 36% had been arrested, 70% ticketed, and 90% harassed.

From a human-interest perspective, the criminalization of homelessness is clearly bad politics. It dehumanizes people and perpetuates both poverty and suffering. But these policies are also bad public health.

A medical anthropologist-turned-freelance journalist, I propose a 2,500-word article illustrating how anti-homeless policy creates and exacerbates public health issues by:

• Making outreach harder,

• Encouraging drug use, even among folks who want to quit and

• Aggravating pre-existing mental health conditions.

In turn, these policies actually cost our communities. I'll draw upon my own 4+ years of research with homeless methamphetamine users in northern Colorado and interviews with scholars of poverty and housing insecurity.

To bridge the gap between academic research and lay understandings of drug use and poverty, I have written personal and guest blog posts. I am currently working on a graphic novel showcasing the stories of several long-term key informants.

I've linked to relevant clips below and peer-reviewed articles are available upon request.

The Joy of Giving: Emotion as Rationality in the Moral Economies of Survival, at *Somatosphere: Science, Medicine, and Anthropology*

Danger/Security in Drug Research, at Alcohol, Drugs, and Tobacco Study Group

Putting a Roof Over One's Head on my blog, *An Anthropology of the Familiar*

Thank you for your time and consideration.

All the best,

Stacey McKenna

Here is a query from freelance writer Amanda Castleman that went to *Sierra* magazine. It resulted in the article "Looking for the Real Silent Night": www.sierraclub.org/sierra/2016-6-november -december/explore/looking-for-real-silent-night. Amanda opens with a personal note reminding the editor of their connection at a recent conference. She then proceeds to set the scene of this quiet camping area. Following the intro, she moves into why this piece is relevant now and how it will impact readers. She ends with a link to her website and a short list of recently published clips.

Hi [redacted],

Lovely to see you in Vancouver at Travel Classics [a travel writing conference]! We spoke about a potential story about Christmas camping (a holiday tweak on my BBC coverage). I've sketched out a few details below.

Please let me know if this has any appeal, and I'll air out my backpacking gear so I can report this in December for 2016 coverage!

THE MOST SILENT NIGHT

A hiker camps in America's quietest place: a sound sanctuary among the ancient cedars and moss-shrouded spruces of Olympic National Park in Washington State. The One Square Inch of

Silence—created by Emmy-winning acoustic-ecologist Gordon Hempton—protects the natural soundscape in the western hemisphere's best and largest swath of virgin temperate rainforest.

Why now: amid the bustle and increasing commercialism of the holiday season, this story would remind people to reconnect with nature's serenity, even in colder climates. Also, activists hope to make this area the world's first official quiet zone; the sonic equivalent of a Dark Sky Reserve, by the park system's centennial in 2016.

My portfolio is online at www.amandacastleman.com. Some articles of special interest may include:

BBC—"Eyeball to Eyeball with Canada's Migrating Salmon"
Travelgirl Magazine—"Guyana: Running Naked in Paradise"
Road & Travel Magazine—"Calm As The Hurricane's Eye" (won a Lowell Thomas for adventure writing)

Many thanks for your consideration.

Cheers,
Amanda

Queries can feel daunting at first, but if you follow the steps outlined here, you will find success. The hope is the more you write them, the more comfortable you get with the process. Queries can begin to feel a little formulaic, and that is a good thing. You want to find a system that works for you and even get to the point where you create a basic template to follow each time you sit down to write a query. Then you have the basic structure and all that is needed is the personalization for each magazine.

QUERY CHECKLIST

____ Does it have a good hook?
____ Is the writing tight?
____ Is the purpose of the article clear?
____ Does your writing show confidence?

_____ Is your bio paragraph strong?
_____ Did you find the correct editor to send the query to?
_____ Did you proofread your query for errors?
_____ Do you have your contact information on the query?

Article Example: Q&A

INSIDE THE QUERY PROCESS, WITH CHILDREN'S EDITOR MARILYN EDWARDS

Although writing for younger audiences isn't that much different than writing for other markets, there are some nuances to it that are good to know. To find out more about this I reached out to industry expert Marilyn Edwards, who has been a children's magazine editor since the early nineties. She has been the editor-in-chief for *Hopscotch for Girls, Boys' Quest,* and *Fun For Kidz* magazines. As a former school music teacher, she brought all her experiences working with children into the magazine world. Here is a Q&A with her to give you more insight into this genre of magazine writing.

1. What do you look for in a query or submission that will make you say "yes"?

Since our issues are around themes, I am first looking to see if the query or submission might be something that we could use in one of our themes. I look for a nonfiction piece that would lend itself to photo support. If it is about a person doing something, then we need good photo support from the author. I am also looking for something new that we haven't used before. That is why working it around an individual, as opposed to an article on an animal or a place, etc., is probably something we have already used at some point. We have 30 years of material to choose from, as well as writers in-house, so general items are things we can fill easily. The *best* ideas are things with kids; but the kids need to be no younger than eight as our target reading level is 8 to 10-year-olds. We have had submissions come in with photos of kids but the kids are very young. That doesn't work with our audience. Also, our themes are listed on our website.

That is also not to discourage someone from sending in something that doesn't fit a theme. If it is a fresh idea, something new and different, I will hold it to see if I can come up with a future theme to use it in. Again, I am speaking about nonfiction.

2. What do you wish more adults understood about writing for the children's market?

Unless the target audience is preschool or 5–6-year-olds, most children's editors are not interested in fiction stories with animals as the characters. *Fun For Kidz* stays away from most holidays, as that is dated material, and our themes are not time sensitive with the exception of the seasons, on occasion.

A few mistakes I have observed from new writers:

1.) Not having looked at the magazine they are sending in a submission for.

2.) Not proofreading their submission.

3.) Not checking that their cover letter is directed to the magazine. I have occasionally seen a cover letter written to another magazine and included as the letter to our magazine.

4.) For me, I hate to not have the word count listed on the manuscript. I don't have time to count the words.

5.) Being in a hurry to get something in the mail and not checking the above items. Some writers use the shotgun approach to send their story out to lots of publishers. But if they haven't done their homework, it is a wasted effort. The writer needs to know that this article would be a great fit for a particular magazine because, having looked at issues, read the guidelines, and given themselves lots of lead time—months, it might have a chance.

The biggest advice I can offer to writers is to research a magazine they like, then find a niche. We once had a great article with great photos of a elementary-age girl visiting a baby bear in hibernation. This was, of course, with park rangers. I don't recall the story, but the photos were fantastic. This author sent it to a few publishers, and it was grabbed QUICK. It had a child of the right age doing something really unusual. Not everyone is going to find that sort of thing but it is important to think outside the box. It is the unusual that gets attention.

3. How long do you usually spend reading a query letter?

Fortunately I read fast. I read a letter, then try to respond immediately unless I have to research the answer.

4. What is the process after you find a submission that interests you? Do you immediately reach back out to the writer, or do you take the idea to an editorial team?

Often something comes in that might work for a future issue, but until we are working on that issue, I don't have an answer. If it is something that I know immediately we will want to use sometime in the future, we respond to the writer ASAP. Otherwise, my assistant editor and I look it over and determine whether it will work, and at that point we let the author know. If something does not work, we send those back immediately.

5. I assume you have some favorite freelance writers you work with. What are the common qualities of these writers?

They know our magazine, send in items that might work, and have proofread the article. They send in nonfiction with photo support, or it is a topic for which we can obtain our own photo support.

6. What do writers need to know when creating and submitting fillers, like puzzles and crafts?

They need to target our target reading level—8 to 10-year-olds. We do include a couple of puzzles that a younger child could do. The other important thing is to look at our theme list on our website.

7. Anything else you want to add?

We appreciate everyone who sends in manuscripts. If they check our theme list and focus on nonfiction especially with older children (7 and up), the chances are greater that we will be able to find a place for the article. Also, length is important—keep to about 300 words or so for one page. We will not usually schedule something that takes up more than two pages.

CHAPTER FIVE

• • •

CONTRACTS & RIGHTS

You have done your research, studied the market, written an amazing query or article, and now you have been offered an assignment! It's a perfect time to stop for a moment and celebrate before moving on to the next phase of the process.

Once you are done dancing around, it's time to get to work—no, not writing the article yet! The first order of business is looking over the contract the editor sent you. Set aside some time so you can read it carefully.

Some contracts are lengthy and detailed, others are short and simple, but they still cover the pertinent information. Occasionally with smaller publications you may not get a formal contract, so you need to create an agreement with the editor (more details on how to do this later in the chapter).

The key to reading through a contract is to take it slow. It may seem complicated but if you take it piece by piece, you will see it's pretty straightforward. I suggest printing out a copy. Then sit down with a highlighter or colored pencil to underline the key points in the contract. You want to make sure you understand what you are signing, not blindly trusting that you will agree with everything in the contract. No matter how excited you are about the assignment, read it over carefully.

The main components in a contract include:

- payment
- rights
- reprints
- deadline
- word count

These are all important to understand before you sign anything. Let's look at these more closely so you can understand the different pieces that make it up and feel confident signing or negotiating the contract. Here are questions to consider before you sign.

WHAT IS THE PAYMENT?

The amount you get paid for an article can vary from five cents a word up to two dollars or more per word. Some publications may offer a flat rate for the article and not a per-word payment. It isn't that one is better than the other, it is two different ways of approaching it.

Different factors go into determining the amount being offered. Bigger publications have bigger budgets, your experience is taken into account, the amount of research needed to write the article, and your history with the publication (how often you have written for them in the past).

Zac Petit, author of *The Essential Guide to Freelance Writing* and former editor at *Print*, explains his process for determining the amount to offer a freelancer for an assignment in *Print*.

"When I'm planning an issue for *Print*, I first look at the amount of editorial pages I have to play with (all the pages that aren't set aside for advertising). Then I look at my set budget for the issue (which we negotiate with our publisher once a year). Then I factor in our regular per-word pay rate, which influences both how many articles I can acquire and how long each article will be. I pay authors as much as I can afford to give them. Editors often find themselves in a use-it-or-lose-it budget scenario, where they want to spend their full budgets so that those budgets aren't lowered the next year."

Because you are a freelancer and basically an independent contractor for the magazine, you will probably be asked to fill out a W-9 form as well. Then at the end of the year you will receive a 1099 tax form stating how much you were paid and letting you know this amount was submitted to the IRS. Then you are responsible for the taxes on that money.

Is it worth it?

Once you see the rate you are being offered, you need to decide if it is worth the time and effort it will take to write the article. You may be offered five-hundred dollars for a fifteen-hundred-word article, and that initially sounds great, but maybe you are being asked to interview a number of different people and travel is involved. You guess it is going to take you about thirty hours to pull it all together. That gives you an hourly rate of about sixteen dollars. For another article, maybe you are being offered twenty-five cents per word for one thousand words. That's only $250, but it is a topic you know a lot about and you estimate it will take you about ten hours to complete. Now you will get about twenty-five dollars per hour.

Will you be able to repurpose or sell again?

Think about whether you will be able to sell the article again to another publication as a reprint or whether you can use the same basic information with some additional material and create a brand-new article. Many local parent magazines will accept full articles, and you don't even have to query. The downside is they don't pay very much, usually around twenty-five to fifty dollars per article. But they also don't compete with each other, so you can send the same article to dozens of these and offer them one-time rights. Let's say it takes you three hours to write a five-hundred-word article and then another hour to find the contact info for the markets. If you sell it to one publication for thirty dollars, you will get about seven dollars per hour for your time. But if you send it to fifteen markets and six of them buy it, totaling $165, then you have bumped up your hourly rate to forty dollars.

Does it help your credentials?

Sometimes writing for a popular publication (either print or online) that doesn't pay well can help boost your bio and credentials. I am not advocating writing for free, but some reputable places, especially online, have a low pay rate. They would be great to include in your bio though, as you build your credentials. So in this case it could be worth it to write for them, even though you might get less than minimum wage.

How much editing will it require?

This is difficult to know if you haven't worked with a particular editor before, but once you have, you can use this to help determine if the pay rate being offered is fair. Revising a piece based on the editor's suggestions is part of business and should be expected. But if you know a certain editor requires a lot of time and energy from you during the revision process, then take that into account. All the editors I have worked with have been wonderful. With some, I send in the final article, they make some minor edits, then I see it when it is published. Others want me to rework a small section, have questions about the facts, or want me to add more. We go back and forth a couple of times, then it is complete. It has never been too time consuming. But I have a good idea of what to expect with each editor after I work with him once.

Will it lead to other assignments?

Maybe you are being offered an assignment and the pay is a little low for you, but this is the first time you have written for this publication, and you believe it will lead to other assignments. By taking this one, you have the opportunity to prove to the editor that you can do a great job and you are easy to work with. Then when you are offered another assignment, you are in a position to negotiate a higher pay rate.

Will you enjoy it?

In most cases you will have queried to get the assignment, and I assume you are not querying about topics you have no desire to write about. There may be instances though, after you have written for a publication or blog, where the editor may ask you to write about a specific topic. If it is a subject you don't know a lot about or have no desire to write about it, then it may be best to pass on the assignment. You want to be able to do a great job, and if it is something you won't enjoy at all, that may show up in the writing and might not reflect well on you and your work.

I once worked for a company that provided blog content to other businesses. It was my job to write posts on a variety of topics. I did well on most of the assignments, but when I was asked to write about a supply chain management company, I couldn't wrap my head around exactly what they did and how it worked. I researched and found out that this type of company oversees materials, information, and finances as they move in a process from supplier to manufacturer to wholesaler to retailer to consumer, plus coordinates and integrates these flows both within and among companies. I had the basic gist of what they did, but I had to spend a lot of time reading and learning more and trying to figure out how to translate that information into something beneficial for their audience. I wrote one post, but I finally had to tell the editor I couldn't do any more posts on this topic. It wouldn't be fair to the company if I kept trying to write about something I didn't fully comprehend, and I was getting frustrated because I didn't understand the subject. Plus it was using up time that I could spend on other writing.

WHAT ARE THE RIGHTS BEING OFFERED?

The rights you are selling with the article are a big deal and not something to take lightly. Be sure to understand the rights being offered and negotiate if necessary.

- First North American Serial Rights: This gives the magazine the exclusive rights to be the first to publish your article. It means that until that article is published (and usually for ninety days after), you can't do anything else with it. Once that time frame is up, then you can send it to other places.
- One-Time Rights: This gives the publication the right to publish your piece one time, but you retain the rights to it.
- Second Serial Rights (Reprint Rights): This gives the publication the nonexclusive rights to publish a piece that has already been published somewhere else. They are buying the right to publish it one time. The pay for a reprint is ten to fifty percent of what the magazine would normally pay for first-time rights.
- All Rights: As the name implies, you are selling the magazine all rights to the article. And this means forever. You can no longer sell that piece (as it appeared published) anywhere else. It doesn't mean they have the rights to the idea, so if you have other articles you want to write on a similar topic, that's fine as long as the final pieces are vastly different. Avoid giving up all rights to your work if you can. You need to weigh the benefits before accepting these terms. Do you feel it is something you can sell again? Are you being offered a lot of money for the article? Is it a magazine

that will boost your credentials? Take all of this into consideration before signing away all your rights. I once wrote an article for a national women's magazine, and when I got the contract I noticed they bought all rights. They were paying well for the piece, and I figured it would be a good publication to add to my résumé. So I signed the contract. The editor warned me that she and her team made lots of changes and edits to the articles they commissioned. I turned in the piece, received my money, and when I saw the final result in print, I didn't recognize any of it. They had taken the basic concept I sent and completely reworked it. The byline was my name along with one of their editors. I was disappointed because I couldn't use it as a clip to show my writing style to future editors. But then I remembered they bought the rights to what was printed, not the idea or what I had submitted to them. I took the original piece I sent to them and sent it to Chicken Soup for the Soul, and it was published in one of their anthologies. In the end, it all worked out.

- Electronic Rights: The rights to publish the article on a variety of media platforms including websites, CDs, DVDs, video games, apps, and more. If nothing is specified in the contract, the rights remain with you.

When will you get paid?

There are two standard times to get paid for your article: on acceptance or on publication. On acceptance is the better option. Once any revisions are made and the editor accepts the article, you get paid. It usually happens within thirty to sixty days. When a magazine pays on publication, you get your money after the article is published. This may not be for a few months, so there could be a big lag from when you submit the final article to when you see your payment.

What is a kill fee?

Many contracts include a kill fee, though some smaller publications don't. This means that if for some reason the editor decides not to run your piece, you will get some compensation for your time. Typically it is around twenty-five percent of what was originally agreed on. An article can be killed for a variety of reasons. It might be that what you wrote doesn't fit with the magazine's editorial vision, and the editor doesn't feel a rewrite is going to fix it. Maybe things have changed in the world and the topic is no longer relevant, or maybe there were changes at the magazine, and there is no longer space for the article. Regardless, you will get paid the kill fee.

DEADLINE AND WORD COUNT

The contract should specify the deadline when you need to turn in the finished article to the editor and the word count expected for your piece. Before you sign anything, make sure you can honor both of these. Editors are under a tight schedule for each issue, and you need to respect that by getting your article in on time. When it comes to word count, especially for print, you need to stick as close to the number as you possibly can. I always consider it a fun challenge to try to get the number exact.

Negotiating

If there is something in the contract you don't agree with, whether the rights being offered, the payment or something else, it's okay to bring it up to the editor and start a dialogue. The editor is not going to take the assignment away because you have questions or want to discuss changing something in the contract terms. Be professional and respectful.

Payment and rights are two areas I negotiate the most. If a publication wants all rights, I will ask for that to be changed. Payment is another place I negotiate. I have found editors are always open to discussing the payment. There are times when they are maxed out on their budget and can't offer any more. If I have written for a magazine before and the editor was pleased with my work, I will ask for more money with the next assignment. I have also asked for more money when I felt the amount of work needed to complete the piece warranted a higher rate. If the editor won't accept your changes, then you have to decide if it is worth it for you.

Create a Contract

If the editor does not send a formal contract, ask if there is one you can sign. If not, then you create an e-mail with all the terms in it. I have had this happen quite a few times, and it isn't anything to be alarmed about. This will help clarify what you are being expected to do and will make sure you and the editor are both on the same page, and the e-mail becomes the contract. Include deadline, word count, payment, and rights being offered. Make sure the editor replies to the e-mail and agrees with what you included.

Contracts are part of the business and are meant to cover both the publisher and writer. Read through them carefully to understand what you are signing and respectfully speak up if you have questions or don't agree with something. It won't take long before you feel confident in reading and understanding these legal documents.

REPRINTS

Writing an article and then being able to resell it to another market as a reprint is a fantastic way to get the most out of your hard work. Why not continue to make money off your piece? Most writer's guidelines will state whether they accept reprints. Smaller local and regional magazines are great places to start. Instead of querying, you need to write a cover letter that explains when and where the article was originally published and what rights you are offering (one-time rights). You then include the article in the body of the e-mail unless the guidelines say attachments are acceptable. As mentioned earlier you will get ten to fifty percent of what the magazine pays for first-time rights.

Usually you offer a reprint to publications other than the one it was originally published in. Sometimes the same one wants to use it again and will pay you to reprint the article. I have an article, "How to Find Success in the Magazine World," that has been in the past five *Writer's Markets*. The editor originally bought one-time rights, and the right to publish it in the future for a reprint rate. Each year it runs again, I get a nice check in the mail.

A FEW TIPS FROM A LAWYER

Attorney Diane J. Cohen, Esq., shared her insight and expertise regarding a few areas of concern to freelance writers. She explained that most legal issues are not simple yes or no answers because they depend on the specific circumstances around that one event or situation.

Cohen graduated from Rutgers Law School (New Jersey) in May 1982 and was admitted to practice in Colorado, Massachusetts, and New Jersey. She has served as a civil attorney, criminal defense attorney, and prosecutor (assistant district attorney, Middlesex County, Massachusetts). Currently she practices on a part-time basis, including pro bono and volunteer work with the Larimer County Bar Association on the committee for Free Legal Clinic for Veterans and as a volunteer attorney at the clinics.

Please note: This information, originally published in *2015 Children's Writer's & Illustrator's Market*, is provided as a favor, for basic understanding of general principles, and does not represent legal advice, nor is it intended for the purpose of guiding any legally consequential action or choice, and that no attorney-client relationship has been established. It's always best to consult a legal expert if you have specific questions pertaining to your work.

If a freelance job is offered through e-mail and there is no official contract, can an e-mail spelling out the terms of the agreement work, and will it be seen as a legal document?

Yes, but be certain all terms of the spelled out agreement are clear, unequivocal, and acceptance also clear and unequivocal. Best to have the parties include within the agreement that both parties have agreed to do same by e-mail and that a copy will be initialed/signed by each and scanned, and each will have a fully executed copy, which will serve as original and be accepted as same. This is not unusual.

Some writers are concerned they will pitch an idea to an editor, then the editor will tell them no and assign the article to another writer. What can a writer do to prevent something like this from happening?

Choose a reputable editor. ... There are thieves in all walks and fields. Note that *anything* in writing is actually subject to copyright protection, even if it is not registered with the copyright office; but it's hard (nearly impossible) to prove *unless* it is registered. Ideas can't be registered and, unless fully fleshed out, are hard to protect or assert are protected. (What are *West Side Story* or *The Fantasticks* but versions of *Romeo and Juliet*?). There are entire courses at law school covering this matter. It's best to know who you are working with, because even if you can prove it, do you really want to go through the experience of suing?

UNDERSTANDING FAIR USE

According to Diane J. Cohen, Esq., "Fair use" is a legal term for matters subject to copyright protection. Fair use is intended for educational use (limited portions sufficient to address the matter to be learned or discussed) and review (e.g., book review, critique), or satirical use (like Weird Al Yankovic). If something is used for educational purposes or review, the portions copied or quoted must indicate a source and attribute. ...

Fair use does not mean a writer can use a certain percentage of someone else's work. Song lyrics are commonly used in all kinds of writing. People justify it by saying they took only one line of the song. It doesn't matter how much you use, you need permission or you are violating copyright laws.

If you are researching an article online and you find great information for your topic, don't assume you can pull the text verbatim, cite the source, and that's all you need to do. To be on the safe side, you should look into getting permission from the original writer.

CHAPTER SIX

WRITING THE ARTICLE

Congratulations! After all your hard work and writing the perfect query, you now have an assignment. The editor has detailed the word count, deadline, the rights, and the payment, now it's time to write the article. Keep in mind everything you learned when you studied the magazine: the style, the tone, the use of quotes. You will now put it to good use.

If this is all still new and you aren't sure how to begin, a formal outline is a good place to start. An outline can save you a lot of time in the long run because it will give you a structure to follow and help you stay on track.

CREATING AN EFFECTIVE OUTLINE

Outlining is an effective tool for organizing the information you collected for your article. It helps break down the content into manageable pieces and allows you to get a general feel for the flow of the article. Think back to your school days when you had to create outlines for a five-paragraph essay. Here is a quick refresher.

First look through your research material and pull out the points most relevant to the information you promised to cover in your query letter. These become your main headings. Under these, create at least two subheadings; then if you have more details you want to include, add at least two subheadings under those. This ensures you have enough content for that section.

Heading (main point)

1. Subheading 1 (point giving more detail about main heading)
2. Subheading 2
    a. Next level of subheading (more detail about subheading 2)
    b. Another level of subheading
        i. You can go even deeper if necessary with more detail about Subheading 2
        ii. Related to Subheading 2

Here is an example of an outline for a feature article I wrote for *Colorado Homes & Lifestyles* about Colorado wineries. You can see how each section is broken down and the basic information for each part is highlighted. I listed facts and other material I wanted to be sure to include. You can be as detailed as you need for this process. For me, I need only key points to remind me of the elements I want to include. You may need more thorough information with complete sentences, quotes, and descriptions. The outline is meant as a guide to help you navigate the article, so create it in a way that is most helpful to you.

Colorado Wineries Article

Title: Think Wine, Think Colorado

1. Introduction
2. Overview of wine industry in Colorado
    a. First winery opened in 1968 by Gerald Ivancie
    b. Vineyards
        i. 96 percent are located on the Western Slope in the Grand River Valley
        ii. High elevation combined with the location of the valley blocks high winds and bad weather

c. Orchard Mesa Research Center
  i. Opened by Colorado State University in 1974
  ii. Continues to research winemaking and provides information to winemakers
3. Colorado Cellars
  a. State's oldest winery opening in 1978 in the Grand Valley
  b. Facts about their wines
    i. 20 varieties of wines
    ii. Produce 10,000 cases annually
  c. They also offer 30 types of wine-based foods

4. Old Town Winery
  a. Owner was a former teacher who made wine on the side for his family
  b. Opened his winery in Old Town Arvada in 1997
    i. Owner considers winemaking an art and takes his time making sure it is well-balanced before bottling it
5. Trail Ridge Winery
  a. Owner began his career selling winemaking and home-brewing supplies
  b. Owner found partners and bought farm in Loveland
  c. Winery opening in 1996

6. Augustina's Winery
  a. Owner is a former geologist
  b. She is dedicated to making wines that go with backpacking, blues music, books, and gingersnaps
  c. She has unique labels for her wines that have won design awards

7. Balistreri Vineyards
  a. Family-owned winery located near Denver

  b. Wine is made with no sulfites or sugar added, and aged in American oak barrels

8. St. Kathryn Cellars
  a. Owned by a retired judge and his wife
  b. Opened in 1999 in Palisade
  c. The large tasting room showcases their wine, but there is also a gift shop, artist corner, and dining area
  d. They have a year-round event center

9. Closing

PRINCIPLES OF STRONG WRITING

Once you are ready to begin writing, there are some strategies to make your article the best it can be. An invaluable source to help you write a fantastic piece is the classic *The Elements of Style* by William Strunk and E.B. White. This "little book" crams a wealth of information into a small amount of space. Since the first printing in 1920, this resource has been a staple among writers and is still as relevant today as it was when it was released. The information about using strong verbs, tight writing, and specific language continues to be helpful to anyone interested in improving their writing skills. Plus, the highbrow humor related to the English language and the misuse of it will make any writer smile.

Mark Garvey, author of *Stylized: A Slightly Obsessive History of Strunk & White's The Elements of Style*, believes in the power of *The Elements of Style* and the message it conveys. In his book he states, "As practical as it is for helping writers over common hurdles, *The Elements of Style* also embodies a worldview, a philosophy that, for some, is as appealing as anything either author ever managed to get down on paper."

Here are some tips from Strunk and White that will help strengthen your writing and give you the tools needed to write solid and effective articles.

Create a Good Flow

"Vigorous writing is concise. A sentence should contain no unnecessary words, a paragraph no unnecessary sentences."

—STRUNK AND WHITE

A good flow will help the reader move seamlessly through your article, guiding her from point to point through various topics. A paragraph is the basic structure of any writing and should be constructed with care. Strunk and White point out, "The object of treating each topic in a paragraph by itself is, of course, to aid the reader. The beginning of each paragraph is a signal that a new step in the development of the subject has been reached."

After you have researched your article and compiled all your data, facts, and information, it's important to arrange it in a practical way for the reader. Big blocks of print can be intimidating for readers. It is helpful to break long paragraphs into smaller ones, even if it isn't necessary because visually it will be more appealing.

In addition to keeping paragraphs manageable in size, another good strategy is to utilize bullet points. These can help your reader navigate through your material with ease and create better understanding of what you are trying to convey.

Using quotes throughout a piece can serve to enhance your points and bring another voice or expert into the mix. Use only the best part of the quote, the part that supports your ideas. Then the reader can easily connect with it and not get bogged down with extraneous information. Sometimes, no matter what you do to guide an interview you end up with a long, unwieldy quote. It may be necessary to paraphrase it to best fit with your article. Use the essence of the quote and attribute it to the person.

During interviews people are sharing their thoughts and insights. They don't always say things in a way that translates well into a written piece. They are talking and that's a different form of communication than writing. Here is an example of the interview I did with Andrew McCarthy about travel writing. This is a section of the actual transcribed conversation:

> Once you find that nugget you can hang the whole story on it and the rest is basically arranging furniture. Once you find your lede, the rest of the story is fine. When you have a strong lede, you're done. Then you write your nut graph while you're there. Then you're done. You write a couple vignettes, they play out. Done. Classic travel writing format. Your lede, your nut graph, your 3 or 4 supporting examples and then you return to your lede at the end. Once you have your lede you can start to enjoy yourself and let the happy accidents begin to happen.

There are some great pieces of information in here, but it doesn't read well. It sounds like someone talking. To create a good flow, I had to lift out a good quote or two and then paraphrase the rest. Here is how the final published piece read:

> Tiny details and incidents capture the essence of a place, believes McCarthy. "Once you find that nugget you can hang the whole story on it," says McCarthy, "and the rest is basically arranging furniture." You follow the lede with a nut graph, three or four supporting examples and then circle back to the lede at the end.

Write Tight

"The surest way to arouse and hold the reader's attention is by being specific, definite, and concrete."

—STRUNK AND WHITE

Editors appreciate writers who turn in succinct, clear articles at the word count assigned. But it is more than the word count that matters; it is the quality of your words that really counts. It is the ability to convey your message and points clearly. When compiling all your notes and information, chances are you will have more than you need. You must dig through it all to find the hidden gems and pertinent material. It may feel overwhelming, and you may think there is no way to pull off an effective article with your allotted word count, but I am here to tell you it is possible.

A few years ago I wanted to take a nine-hundred-word essay I had written and published, and rework it for another publication. The challenge was that I had to cut it to no more than 250 words, yet maintain the essence of the piece, which was that in a few days, I went from being disinterested in fly-fishing to falling in love with it. I wanted to see if I could do it. I read over the piece and began by cutting out unnecessary descriptions, then any sections that didn't support the main message I wanted to convey. I cut and cut and cut, but still needed to eliminate 150 more words. I persisted and eventually I got it down to the needed word count, submitted it, and it was published. This took "writing tight" to a new level and showed me it could be done.

First Article (959 words)

As I stood in the Cache La Poudre River and looked around, I realized I was the only one crazy enough to be out fishing in December. My chest waders kept me dry, but I still felt the freezing temperature of the water on my skin. I lifted my fly line out of the river, gently cast it back and forth a few times before placing it back on the water. Like an addict I needed a hit, but mine involved a fish biting the fly at the end of my line.

A few years ago, if someone had asked me my thoughts on fly-fishing I would have said it looked complicated and boring. I always teased my fly-fishing friends about their obsession with the sport because I didn't understand what the big deal was.

So, two years ago, when I agreed to be a parent chaperone on a week-long fly-fishing trip with my 16-year-old daughter and 20 other students from Polaris Expeditionary Learning School, my fly-fishing friends were surprised. I told them I wasn't going because of the fishing. I agreed to go because I love to cook for people.

The third morning, after feeding everyone a hearty breakfast, I sat on the bank of the river and watched my daughter fish. I admired the ease with which she cast her line into the water, stripped it in as she followed the current, and then did it again. I sat there, under a crystal blue autumn sky, immersed in what she was doing without any awareness that three hours had passed.

Throughout the trip, I was amazed at how the behavior of the usually energetic, hormonal, friend-centered teenagers changed when they got in the river. I watched them not only learn to fish, but learn to be more comfortable in themselves and with the quiet. My perception of fly-fishing shifted, and I knew I wanted to stay connected to this world where time faded away and to-do lists disappeared with the current.

A week after my return, I headed to the Big Thompson with a friend who is an avid angler. Following a crash course in casting, I slipped on the oversized borrowed waders, grabbed my friend's rod and stepped into the river. As I prepared for my first cast on the water, my hand trembled slightly from nerves, and I prayed I would not make a complete fool of myself.

After a quick review from my friend, I concentrated on the cadence of my casting. Each time my fly landed on the water, my insides tightened up in anticipation of a hit. Following a successful cast, my pink indicator bobbed, signaling a bite. I yelled to my friend, but my delay in setting the hook allowed the fish to get away.

As we worked our way upstream, all sense of time drifted downstream. I enjoyed the sunshine, the sound of the river, and being away from the 200 e-mails waiting in my in-box. I persevered for four hours until I finally hooked and reeled in my first fish—an eight-inch brown trout. Every nerve in my body screamed with excitement, and I couldn't stop smiling. After a high five with my friend, I posed for a picture with the fish before releasing it back into the water.

I never imagined I would soon become one of the fly-fishing obsessed, constantly checking the weather and river reports. I invested in all the necessary gear, and I craved time on the river, rearranging my schedule so I could be on the water as much as possible. Fishing is a sport dominated by men. But I soon learned that although women make up only twenty-one percent of the angler population in Colorado, they are an active group. The Colorado Women Fly Fishers is a nonprofit organization whose purpose is to encourage and support women who fly fish.

I was thrilled to learn there was a Northern Colorado chapter with more than fifty members. During my first meeting, the room at the local fly shop filled with kindred spirits. While enjoying wine, cheese, and chocolate, the group of women shared fishing stories, tips, and we practiced tying different knots.

I asked a couple of them what they enjoy most about the sport. Julia Houx, co-owner of St. Peter's Fly Shop, loves spending time outside, and fishing is a pastime that allows her to forget about all the other things happening in her life. Plus, she finds it exhilarating to watch a fish come to the surface to eat the fly she just placed on the water. Gretchen Osborn, the meeting organizer, said she is drawn to the sport by the constant challenge coupled with peace and serenity.

Fly-fishing is a sport that takes more precision and finesse than power, making it an activity women of all ages can enjoy and even excel at. Fishing guides have told me it is easier to teach women to fly-fish than men because women tend to be better listeners, and they do not try to overpower the rod.

As I approach my two-year fly-fishing anniversary in October, I am grateful that fishing found me. It brings more balance to my life and helps me be a better version of myself. When I am in a river and the water is flowing all around me, I feel at peace and it calms my busy mind. But that's not enough. I need the adrenaline rush that comes with catching a fish: from setting the hook, to landing the fish in the net, to releasing it in the water. This is what makes my whole body smile, what calls me back to the river, even in the middle of December.

Second Article (235 words)

Fly-fishing is a favorite pastime for many Coloradans, but for me it always looked complicated and like too much work. I had friends who loved it—in fact, were obsessed with it. So, it was a surprise to these same friends that I agreed to be a parent chaperone on a week-long fly-fishing trip with twenty-one students from my daughter's high school.

We traveled from Fort Collins to a private ranch outside of Kremmling. Our camp, high up on a hillside, overlooked a pristine river, meandering its way through the valley. Blue sky and sunshine welcomed us and stayed for the duration of our trip.

After breakfast one morning, I went with my daughter's group to the river. The teacher put her in a spot in the water, gave her a few tips and moved on to the next student. For three hours, I watched her cast and try to set the hook on a few fish. As I sat there in the sun, listening to the river and watching my daughter, the rest of the world disappeared and a peace came over me that I hadn't felt for a long time. I wasn't thinking of work or my to-do list. I was completely in the moment. And in that moment, I knew, fly-fishing would become part of my life.

To tighten your writing, avoid vague language and empty words. For instance, the phrases *the truth is* or *the fact is* are not needed. Strunk and White say, "If you feel you are possessed of the truth, or of the fact, simply state it. Do not give advance billing."

Vague words dilute your writing and weaken the points and information you are conveying. William Zinsser in his book *On Writing Well* states, "Don't say you were a bit confused and sort of tired and a little depressed and somewhat annoyed. Be confused. Be tired. Be depressed. Be annoyed. Don't hedge your prose with timidities. Good writing is lean and confident."

Once you get your initial ideas down on the page, it is good to go back and rid your article of these unnecessary or repeated words and phrases. It strengthens your writing and your reader will appreciate it.

EMPTY WORDS AND PHRASES

Try	Might
Just	Consider ...
Really	Entertain a notion
Very	Hope to
A lot	Would like to ...
Basically	I believe ...
Quite	In my opinion ...
Maybe	I feel ...
Possibly	As far as I can tell ...
Perhaps ...	I suppose ...
With luck ...	I suggest that
The fact is	I think

VARY SENTENCE STRUCTURE

A well-written piece is more than just stringing together a series of words into sentences and paragraphs. You want to create a flow and rhythm for the reader. A paragraph with all long sentences is cumbersome to read; on the other hand, one with only short sentences feels choppy. A combination of the two is best to create an effective fluency for your reader. It breaks up the monotony and presents the information in an easy-to-follow format.

Here is an example. Read the passage, then go back and look at the different types and lengths of sentences.

> Write short. Write tight. Writing and publishing short stories in anthologies, literary journals, and magazines is a fantastic way to strengthen your writing skills and build your publishing credentials. There are many publications on the lookout for well-written short pieces.

Short personal stories are the mainstay for publications like *Chicken Soup for the Soul* and *Brevity*. With more than 250 titles and counting, the Chicken Soup for the Soul series has sold more than 110 million copies in the United States and Canada, and more than 500 million worldwide, making it the best-selling trade paperback series of all time.

Notice in this example the first paragraph opens with two short sentences, followed by a longer sentence, before ending with a short basic sentence. The second paragraph has only two sentences, with the first one being basic while the last one is longer, more involved. There is a good variety of length as well as how the sentences begin. They don't all start with the same structure: noun then verb. One sentence starts with a verb, one with a noun, and one even has a preposition. The point is, there is a variety, making it flow better for the reader.

USE STRONG VERBS

"The active voice is usually more direct and vigorous than the passive."

—STRUNK AND WHITE

Strong verbs make all the difference in your writing. Zinsser believes, "Verbs are the most important of all your tools. They push the sentence forward and give it momentum. Active verbs push hard: passive verbs tug fitfully."

Passive verbs are a weak form that slows down readers and clutters writing. Instead of writing, *The milk had been knocked over by a cat*. Change it to, *The cat knocked over the milk*. The words, *had been* are unnecessary and end up dragging the sentence out.

Passive: The birds were being watched by Susan.

Active: Susan watched the birds.

Passive: A great number of dead leaves were left lying on the ground.

Active: Dead leaves covered the ground.
Passive: Jordan was run down by the bull.
Active: The bull gored Jordan.

The word *was* is called a helping verb and is a common word to identify passive voice. If you have sentences with this word, see if they can be made more active. Here is a complete list of helping verbs that often create passive or weak sentences: am, is, are, was and were, being, been, be.

In contrast, here is a list of strong verbs to use instead of more bland or passive ones.

STRONG VERBS

abolish	change	draft
accelerate	clarify	drive
achieve	clobber	eliminate
act	collaborate	employ
adopt	confront	enable
advise	connect	enlist
align	conquer	ensure
allocate	convert	establish
anticipate	convince	evaluate
apply	create	execute
arbitrate	critique	expand
attain	decide	exploit
avoid	defuse	explore
balance	deliver	fabricate
bellow	demonstrate	facilitate
boost	demystify	filter
break	deploy	finalize
bridge	design	focus
build	develop	forecast
burn	diagnose	foresee
calculate	discover	formulate
capture	divert	gain

gather	manage	resist
generate	master	respond
grasp	maximize	retain
guide	measure	scan
handle	mobilize	shatter
hypothesize	modify	sidestep
identify	monitor	simplify
ignite	motivate	slash
illuminate	negotiate	solve
imagine	overcome	stimulate
implement	penetrate	stretch
improve	persuade	succeed
increase	pinpoint	supplement
innovate	position	synthesize
inspect	prepare	transfer
inspire	prevent	transform
integrate	profit	transplant
intensify	project	unbridled
interfere	recite	unearth
judge	reconsider	unify
jump	reduce	unleash
justify	refresh	unravel
lecture	replace	usher
leverage	report	

BE SPECIFIC

"Prefer the specific to the general, the definite to the vague, the concrete to the abstract."

—STRUNK AND WHITE

Vague words weaken your writing. Specific words provide definition and clarity, making your piece stronger.

You can say, "Bad weather set in for a while."

Or you can be more specific, giving your reader a clearer picture: "It rained every day for a week."

The number of words in each of these examples is exactly the same. But in the first one we are unclear what the *bad weather* is and *a while* can mean different time spans for different people. By saying, *it rained every day for a week*, there is no guess as to the meaning.

Here is a sentence from an article I wrote for a local magazine.

> Across the Big Thompson River and along the bend on Highway 34 toward Estes Park is a fantastic little furniture store that deserves a visit.

Because I wanted people to understand where this store was in relation to the town, I included specific details. I could have said something like "On the outskirts of town, heading toward the mountains, is a fantastic little furniture store," but the locals reading this still wouldn't have a good idea of the area I was referring to. By including detailed landmarks, anyone who lives in the area will know exactly the location I am talking about without including an address.

CHECK YOUR FACTS

The Internet is the first place most of us go to find facts. But as we all know, just because something is on the Internet doesn't mean it is true. It is important to double-check information with multiple sources. Libraries have great resources and links to academic journals and reputable sources on their websites. Use these to ensure the information you are including in your article is accurate.

Other great sources are resource librarians. These wonderful individuals have been trained to research and find information, and they enjoy doing it. You can go in and talk with the librarian, call on the phone, or ask your question online. My library district has a great website and on the site is a link to "ask a librarian." All I need to do is click on that link and type in my research question. A librarian usually gets back to me within twenty-four hours with valuable facts, data, and links. It is an invaluable resource every writer should use.

INTERVIEW TIPS

Getting information from primary sources through interviews can enhance the depth of an article. It adds a level of credibility and strengthens the points you are covering in your piece; and depending on the publication, citing experts may be an integral part of the magazine's style. Depending on your topic and the scope of your article, you many need to interview more than one person to get different insights. Interviews can be done on the phone, in person, and through e-mail. It will depend on the situation as to which option is best.

In-Person and Phone Interviews

When writing a profile, your focus is on one person. For this type of in-depth piece, arrange an in-person meeting or a phone interview. You need to be able to ask follow-up questions and make a connection with the person, which is difficult to do via e-mail.

Research Your Subject

After you set up your appointment to meet, it is time to prepare for the interview. Research the subject and find out as much as you can about her. This way you can spend your time during the interview asking more pointed questions and not take up a lot of time with basic inquiries. Your subject will appreciate it, and it will show her you value her time, and your final piece will benefit.

Years ago I was being interviewed by a local newspaper about an annual writers conference I hosted. The reporter wanted to talk with me about it and get my insight into the event. Unfortunately she spent the first ten minutes or so asking me questions to which the answers could be found on my website. She asked me how long the conference had been going on, where it was taking place, and other surface-level questions. She could have used that time to dig a little deeper. She could have asked, "I read that your conference has been going on for seven years now. Why do you think it has been so successful and continues to be a draw for writers?" A question like this makes me think and get to the core of the event and what makes it tick.

Kevin Vaughan, an award-winning investigative reporter for KUSA-TV 9NEWS in Denver, who also previously reported for the *Rocky Mountain News, The Denver Post,* and FOX Sports, agrees. "Learn everything you can about the person. I find all I can in articles and social media. I think about what I would want to know that I hadn't read anywhere. If I am profiling someone I will try to interview other people before I interview the subject. I like to hear stories from other people and get them to talk about the subject. I think about what the story is and maybe how I am going to present it because this might lead to how I ask questions."

Do your research and create meaningful, thoughtful questions. A couple of days before your scheduled time, reach out to remind your subject about the interview, then also give her a heads-up about the direction you plan to take with the questions and the type of information you are looking for. You don't need to give her all your questions, but at least this way, she will have an idea of what to expect.

Recording and Transcripts

Recording the interview is a good idea. You can do this with an app on your phone or invest in an inexpensive digital recorder. Before I begin, I always ask the subject if he minds if I record the session so that I make sure I get his information and quotes correct. I have never had anyone say no. I also jot down some general notes during the interview just in case something happens with the recording. There are different laws in each state regarding asking permission to record; know what those laws are.

I always transcribe each interview so I have it available when I write the article. Plus it's a good way for me to evaluate how I did as the interviewer. Greg Campbell, a documentary filmmaker, journalist, and best-selling nonfiction author, agrees with the importance of transcripts. "If you come through with a bunch of hogwash from your transcripts, you need to think about whether you are asking the right questions. Because you can see the stage at which you, as an interviewer, screwed up and let it go off the rails."

Be Quiet

During the interview you want to be personable and have some back and forth, but your job is to ask questions, then *listen*. You are there to learn about your subject, not the other way around.

Both Vaughan and Campbell have the same piece of advice, "Shut the hell up."

Vaughan says that as human beings, silence is kind of scary. "When I was younger I would rush to fill that silence by talking or commenting or asking that next question. But if you can force yourself to be quiet, a lot of times that person will rush to fill that space, that silence, with more words. I have found a lot of the most profound things people say is in that situation: when they have sat and thought for a second and it's quiet. They feel they have to say something."

Campbell believes there is this threshold where suddenly you are not interviewing the subject any longer, but you are now listening. The person feels comfortable with you and opens up. It is like a faucet is turned on and they are ready to talk more freely. "The paradigm shifts a little bit and you have to really know when to shut up. And no matter how uncomfortable it may be, let that silence sit there and grow and gain weight and happen between you, because you hit a milestone when it comes to trust between you and your subject. You can now ask a more penetrating question you were holding back on. Because that person was able to show emotion and show vulnerability, they may be more inclined to answer your question in a more forthright way than if that emotional moment hadn't happened."

Be Respectful

Being genuine in who you are and demonstrating to your interview subjects that you are interested in what they have to say encourages them to share more. Campbell says, "They are really trusting that when they open up about something that is very personal and deeply held to them, or if they are an expert and it is a really important piece of technical information they are going to relay to you, you are going to be able to dutifully and honestly and capably spit it back out the way they intended it to be. That is a lot of responsibility on your shoulders."

When talking with someone about an emotional issue for them, be gentle and respectful. Vaughan says, "Someone might be describing the death of a child. I never say 'I know how you feel' because I don't know how they feel. I think it is kind of condescending to say that. I do try to be a human being and say 'that must have been really awful' or 'that must have been really difficult.'"

If you plan to write about political or controversial topics, there may be times when you must talk with someone who you know has very different opinions and views from you. Don't shy away from talking with this person because it will add another dimension to your article. Even with opposing views, it is possible to be genuine and have a good interview.

Campbell says he suspends his worldview as much as possible and goes into the interview with the idea that he is going to learn something. "I am going to try to be a clean slate and keep an open mind to whatever their perspective is. Especially if it is really different from mine because I am curious about it. I actually think those can be good interviews if you come at somebody, not from a confrontational point of view but from an oppositional point of view. Then you are in a good position to ask them good questions and challenge their perceptions and their beliefs. If you do it in a genuine and honest way, and you want to learn about their perspective and their point of view, I think they will be receptive. It's worked pretty well for me. It's that intellectual honesty of, I want to know what makes you tick. I want to know why you hold these beliefs."

How to Handle Bunny Trails

Sometimes the interview will go in a different direction than what you anticipated. You have two choices at this point. You can gently bring back the focus to the topic you need addressed, or if you feel it might lead to some great information, go with the new direction.

"My instinct is to let the person talk," says Campbell. "In some ways that's been to my benefit because I never know what the next thing is they are going to say. ... If I genuinely don't understand something, or I think I finally get a point they are trying to make, but they are making it over a ten-minute soliloquy, I can say, 'Hold on, I think that's important. Can you go back? Is this what you mean?'"

Anything Else?

End with an open invitation for them to share more. I always end with "Is there anything else you want to add or anything I didn't ask you about that you want to share?" Even though this is the end of the interview, be ready. There have been times when I got amazing answers and insight from my subject at this point. Keep the recorder rolling until you get up and leave the room. You don't want to miss a gold nugget. I also make sure to give my card and let the subject know if he thinks of something he forgot to tell me, he can e-mail or call me. Send a thank-you card or e-mail the next day to let him know you appreciate his taking time to talk with you.

Sharing What You Wrote

Occasionally your subject will ask to see what you write. The standard practice among journalists is to not show the article. You don't want the subject to send you back their edits and suggestions on the whole piece or change his mind and retract what he said. If the person is adamant, you can say it is your policy to not send interview subjects the article before it is published, but you are happy to send the sections with his quotes so he can check for accuracy. (He is not checking for style or whether he likes your writing.) You are under no obligation to send the whole thing.

E-Mail Interviews

There are times when it makes sense to ask your questions via e-mail instead of over the phone. I have done this with many articles when I have a few questions I want to ask a lot of different experts about. It is easier to send them all an e-mail, then have them respond with their answers. You want to make sure you ask detailed questions so the subject understands what you are looking for.

This is an e-mail I sent to seven different literary agents for an article:

> I am writing a Q&A, roundup-style article for the front section of the 2018 *Children's Writer's and Illustrator's Market*, addressing the topic, What Are Agents Really Looking For? I would love to include your insight and expertise. The hope is that by reading the article, writers will be more prepared when seeking representation. If you are open to helping, the questions are below. I need the

answers by Monday, February 6. (If it is easier to do this over the phone, I can arrange that as well.)

Thank you in advance for considering being a part of this article. Kerrie

Questions:

1. In a writer's world, once a manuscript is done, writing a good query can be time consuming and overwhelming, knowing it is the key to getting representation. But in your world, reading queries is a small part of how you spend your time. What catches your eye when it comes to a query, and what makes an effective query?

2. Let's say a writer has written a great query and you request the full manuscript. What typically keeps you reading, and what is something that will stop you right away?

3. What is the biggest mistake adult writers make when writing for young audiences (up through middle grade)?

4. There is lots of talk at conferences and in writing magazines about platform. How important is it to you that a writer have an established platform?

5. What characteristics make up your ideal client?

6. Because picture books are short, some writers think they are easy to write. What is the biggest mistake writers make when writing for this market, and what makes a great picture book?

TOOLS TO HELP WITH INTERVIEWS

TapeACall
    Allows you to record a phone conversation.
    www.tapeacall.com
Dragon Dictation
    Transcribes conversations, making it a great tool to have during an interview.
        www.nuance.com/mobile/mobile-applications/dragon
-dictation.html

STORYTELLING IN NONFICTION WRITING

"Stories are the creative conversion of life itself into a more powerful, clearer, more meaningful experience. They are the currency of human contact."

—ROBERT MCKEE

Storytelling is one of the oldest forms of communication. It's often associated with fiction, but although nearly all articles are nonfiction, storytelling is critical. Whether it is sitting around the dinner table sharing family stories or writing a memoir to put out into the world, we all enjoy telling and hearing a good story. It is a way to pass down history, share common experiences, and ultimately connect us with one another.

Creative nonfiction is all about true events that are written in story form. Memoirs come to mind first. The author shares an experience from her life, but it reads like fiction and has the elements of a story: a good beginning, middle, and end. *The Ledge: An Inspirational Story of Friendship and Survival,* does this well. Originally a serialized feature in a newspaper, this book written by Jim Davidson, an experienced climber, and journalist Kevin Vaughan tells the story of Davidson's climbing accident on Mount Rainier, where he and his climbing partner plunged eighty feet into a crevasse.

> Trapped on a narrow frozen shelf, deep below daylight, he desperately battled crumbling ice, snow that threatened to bury him alive, and crippling fear of the inescapable chasm below—all the while struggling to save his fatally injured friend. Finally, alone, with little equipment and rapidly dwindling hope, he confronted a fateful choice: the certainty of a slow, lonely death or the near impossibility of an agonizing climb for life. A story of heart-stopping adventure, heartfelt friendship, fleeting mortality, and implacable nature, *The Ledge* chronicles the elation and grief, dizzying heights and punishing depths of a journey to hard-won wisdom.

This book reads like a novel and keeps you riveted until the end. Davidson and Vaughan could have written it as straight nonfiction, providing the reader with all the detailed information and facts surrounding the event, but instead they chose to write it as a story.

For Vaughan there was never any doubt that *The Ledge* would be written in a way that reads like fiction. "The experience in story is so much more rich. If you think about it, when we tell each other stories, we do it in a very engaging way."

How does that translate to magazine writing? Why should we use storytelling when the purpose of many articles is to share information? Here are three reasons why storytelling strengthens nonfiction writing.

Provides an Emotional Connection

Sharing stories with family and close friends is a way we connect with them on an emotional level. When we have known someone for a long time, stories are a way we can share common memories and experiences, making us closer and deepening that bond between us. It is all about that emotional connection.

Think about infomercials. The whole concept is based on story. They always pull in lots of stories and experiences from people using and enjoying their product. Rationally we know these are probably actors, but the hope of the advertiser is that it connects with us on an emotional level.

How does that translate into our writing? At times you will want to make an emotional impact on your reader through an article or essay. Years ago I was hired by a marketing company to do just that. An adoption agency hired the firm to help with its marketing. They had a big fundraiser coming up and wanted to make an emotional connection with people to encourage them to come to the event and support their organization. My job was to write a heartfelt article that shared the story of one couple who adopted a baby boy with respiratory issues. The adoption was an open adoption, so the birth mother was going to play some role in the baby's life. I interviewed the couple and the birth mom to provide a well-rounded story that made an emotional impact on the reader.

I opened the article with background on the young single mom who gave birth to a premature baby with health issues and eventually realized she couldn't provide the kind of home the baby needed. She contacted the agency and put him up for adoption. I also shared why the couple decided they wanted to start their family by adopting. I ended the article with this emotional scene:

> The day they got the call that Mandy had chosen them to be Jackson's parents, Vanessa and Brett's life changed forever. Four days after that initial call, the couple met with Mandy, Jackson and his doctor. As Vanessa held the baby, happiness surged through her. She knew in her heart that Jackson was their son.
>
> Two days later Brett and Vanessa went to pick up Jackson at Mandy's house. They spent the day with Mandy's mom and other family members. They talked about Jackson's routine, his medications, his likes and his dislikes. Toward the end of the visit, Mandy's family gathered around him to say their goodbyes. There were tears and even some laughter. When it was time, Mandy placed Jackson in his car seat with love and great care. She hugged him, told him to be strong and that she loved him.
>
> The ride home for Brett and Vanessa was a quiet one filled with mixed emotions. They were thrilled to have their son, but they also understood the immense loss this was for Mandy.
>
> Mandy remains a big part of Jackson's life; she receives pictures and updates from Brett and Vanessa, and visits them as often as possible. Even though she misses him every day, she doesn't regret the loving decision she made.
>
> "He has inspired me to work hard and do something with my life," said Mandy.
>
> In the future Mandy hopes to become a respiratory therapist to help other children with lung problems like Jackson's.

Vanessa and Brett have nothing but respect and admiration for Mandy. They consider her part of their extended family. They strongly believe that it is important for Jackson to always know where he came from.

"It is part of who he is," said Vanessa. "The more people to love one kid, the better."

Sets the Scene

A good story can set the scene for the rest of the article. It gets the reader in the right mind-set for what is coming next. Here is an example from the *The New York Times*. The article was about Henrik Lundqvist, goaltender for the New York Rangers. It sets the scene with a short story before getting into the heart of the article. It provides an interesting introduction to Henrik Lundqvist.

Less than two hours before they were to play the Philadelphia Flyers at Madison Square Garden, the Rangers could not find Henrik Lundqvist. They called his cell phone, but it had been turned off. They called his wife, Therese, who said he had left their Midtown apartment.

On game days, Lundqvist follows an elaborate set of rituals, refined over his years playing in the N.H.L. and in his native Sweden. He knows precisely when he must wake from his nap, when he must eat and when he must arrive at the rink. He listens to the same music, heavy on punk rock, as he tapes his sticks and stretches his limbs. He checks, then double-checks his equipment: his skates, his pads, his gloves. He sits in his stall. He does not talk.

For Lundqvist, to feel unprepared is to feel uncomfortable—and for a goalie, nothing is worse than feeling uncomfortable.

He entered the locker-room as the pregame meeting was about to end. He walked in feeling calm and relaxed. Then he realized that he had miscalculated by an hour. He had only 45 minutes until warm-ups. He did not feel comfortable anymore.

Coach John Tortorella asked Lundqvist if he was ready. Lundqvist said he was. You better be, Tortorella told him.

Anchors a Point

Jack Canfield is a master at using storytelling to anchor a point he wants to get across. In his book *The Success Principles* he weaves intriguing stories throughout the book to help ground the point he is making. For instance, in the chapter "Take 100% Responsibility for Your Life" he talks about the myth in our culture that we are entitled to a great life. He then goes on to talk about how the only person responsible for your quality of life is you. He explains it in more detail, then ends the section with a story, and anchors the point he wanted to make.

He shares an experience he had with W. Clement Stone, a self-made multimillionaire and premier success guru.

> When I was completing my first week's orientation, Mr. Stone asked me if I took 100% responsibility for my life.
>
> "I think so," I responded.
>
> "This is a yes or no question, young man. You either do or you don't."
>
> Well, I guess I'm not sure."
>
> "Have you ever blamed anyone for any circumstance in your life? Have you ever complained about anything?"
>
> "Uh … yeah … I guess I have."
>
> "Don't guess. Think."
>
> "Yes, I have."
>
> "Okay, then. That means you don't take one hundred percent responsibility for your life. Taking one hundred percent responsibility means you acknowledge that you create everything that happens to you. It means you understand that you are the cause of all your experience. If you want to be really successful, and I know you do, then you will have to give up blaming and complaining

and take total responsibility for your life—that means all your results, both your successes and your failures. That is the prerequisite for creating a life of success. It is only by acknowledging that you have created everything up until now that you can take charge of creating the future you want.

"You see, Jack, if you realize that you have created your current conditions, then you can uncreate them and re-create them at will. Do you understand that?"

"Yes, sir, I do."

"Are you willing to take one hundred percent responsibility for your life?"

"Yes, sir, I am!"

And I did.

This example is from a book, but the same thing can be done with an article. You can find a great story to anchor the points you were making in your piece.

TECHNIQUES FOR GOOD STORYTELLING

RELEVANCE: When using storytelling in your articles, make sure the story fits with your topic and adds depth to the points you are making.

CONCISION: Stick to the point and be succinct. Don't ramble and add irrelevant information because you are telling a story.

GOOD CHARACTERS: Every good story has good characters, and that goes for nonfiction too. If you look back at the adoption story example, there was the adoptive mom and dad, the birth mom, and the baby. They all played a role in the story and made it strong.

UNIVERSALITY: This refers to themes and concepts that are universal (love, death, friendship …). When you include these with the storytelling, your reader will be able to better relate to and understand the point you are trying to get across.

THE FIVE SENSES: Good storytelling places the reader in the scene by incorporating as many of the five senses as possible.

FINAL ARTICLE CHECKLIST

_____ Does it have an intriguing title?
_____ Does it have a good lede?
_____ Did you cover all the information promised in the query?
_____ Did you check spelling and punctuation?
_____ Is the word count where it needs to be?
_____ Did you include a short bio?
_____ Did you put your name, e-mail, and page numbers in the footer?

WORKING WITH AN EDITOR

Establishing great working relationships with the different editors is important to your success with magazine writing. You want to be a writer whom editors can rely on to produce quality content on deadline and at the assigned word count. Your reward will be more assignments and quicker access to the editors because they know who you are. Plus if you are reliable, they may reach out to you with assignments.

Deadline and Word Count

As mentioned before, editors are on a tight schedule with each issue. They count on you to turn in your assignment to them on time so they can edit your piece. In addition to honoring the deadline, keep your article to the assigned word count. An editor is given only so much space to work with and if you are way over or under your word count, it will make her job more difficult.

Revision

Another aspect of being that go-to writer is being a good sport when it comes to revisions. Having an editor send back your article for clarification on certain sections and even a few rewrites is part of the process. How much will depend on the editor and your writing. But regardless, you need to take care of any revisions quickly and return them to the editor.

There may be some points you disagree with, and it is fine, in a professional and courteous way, to bring those up and explain why you disagree. Tyler Moss with *Writer's Digest* says, "Sometimes writers like to butt heads with editors over revisions. In some special cases, I'll acknowledge that's warranted, but most of the time I ask writers to recognize that editors have a very clear idea of who their audience is and what the tone of their magazine should be. If editors ask for revisions, don't consider it a personal slight or a commentary on your writing ability—it's just because they want the article to resonate with their audience as much as possible."

Keep the Editor Informed

Keep your editor informed of any problems or issues that may arise. Do this as soon as possible. If you have an interview subject that is critical to the article and is difficult to get in contact with, then let your editor know. Also sometimes life will throw us a curve and events happen that are out of our control. If something comes up and you know you are not going to make your deadline, let your editor know right away.

THESE EDITORS SHARE THE QUALITIES OF THEIR FAVORITE WRITERS

TOD JONES, MANAGING EDITOR FOR *THE COSTCO CONNECTION*: They pitch well. They've researched our online edition to make sure they're not pitching something recently covered. They turn in on time or sooner. The draft is very clean and requires minimal editing.

KATHERINE LAGRAVE, SENIOR DIGITAL EDITOR FOR *CONDÉ NAST TRAVELER*: They turn copy around on time and don't require much editing. They've got the right tone for the publication and voice to their writing, and are telling stories that you can't find anywhere else.

JONAH OGLES, EDITOR FOR *OUTSIDE*: My favorite writers are interested in crafting sentences and stories (even if they sometimes fail). They have a good sense of what makes a story right for *Outside* (even if they sometimes get rejected) and are interested in collaborating (meaning they're not sensitive about being edited but aren't afraid to push back).

KASEY CORDELL, FEATURES EDITOR FOR *5280*: They're reliable reporters and writers with whom I don't have to revise more than a couple of times. They understand our magazine's voice, scope, timeline, and needs. They don't pitch me topics; they pitch fully formed story ideas. They meet deadlines. They hit word counts. They accept edits gracefully and respond appropriately.

TYLER MOSS, EDITOR-IN-CHIEF FOR *WRITER'S DIGEST*: First and foremost, reliability. A reliable contributor turns the completed piece in by the given deadline with (or at least close to) the allotted word count. They're easy to work with through the editing process, primarily because they've followed the plan for the piece we discussed prior to their penning the assignment. However, if the piece does require revisions (and if it does that's okay), they accept the revisions humbly.

MICHELLE THEALL, FORMER SENIOR EDITOR FOR *ALASKA* MAGA-ZINE: My favorite freelancers are reliable. They deliver quality work on time. They have good story ideas, understand the magazine, and turn in clean copy.

ROBBIN GOULD, EDITOR FOR *FAMILY MOTOR COACHING*: I enjoy working with our regular contributors! That's because they know our needs; they communicate clearly; they deliver on time; they submit a complete package following our magazine's parameters; their articles are accurate, relevant, interesting, and well-written. If I know I can rely on a particular writer, I am already receptive; sometimes I'll reach out to her with an article idea.

EDITING APPS AND WEBSITES

WordCounter

In addition to giving you the word count, this program can help you improve your word choice, writing style, and fix grammar mistakes.

www.wordcounter.net

Grammarly

Detects grammar, spelling, punctuation, word choice, and style mistakes in your writing. You can cut and paste your text into the online editor or install the free browser extension.

www.grammarly.com

Hemingway App

By looking at the readability it lets you know how understandable your piece of writing is.

www.hemingwayapp.com

ProWritingAid

Software that analyzes your writing to check for issues, such as grammar mistakes, style, readability, and overused words, and provides suggestions on how to make your writing stronger.

www.prowritingaid.com

CHAPTER SEVEN

• • •

GOAL SETTING

At this point in the book you should have a good understanding of the process of writing for magazines and what it takes to write great articles. Could you venture out now and find some success? Probably. But with a few more tools in your tool kit, you will create a clearer, more direct route and be more productive.

We hear it time and again: We are all given twenty-four hours, but how we use them is up to us. We all know this is true, yet writers frequently tell me they don't have enough time to write. My response, we make time for what is important to us. If writing and publishing magazine articles is important, you will find a way to make it happen. This chapter is about making the best of the time you have for your magazine writing.

When I first started publishing articles, I had a husband, three kids, and was teaching full time. During one of my most productive early years, I sold seven articles. If I were a full-time freelance writer, that would not be good number, but considering my life at the time, it was a fantastic number. Now my kids are grown, and I write and consult with writers full time. What I have found is whether I have five hours a week or forty hours a week to devote to my writing, I need the tools in place to stay organized and productive.

There are challenges with both these scenarios. When I was limited on time, I had to stay focused and organized to meet my deadlines, and I always wished I had a few more hours each week to write. Now that I do have more time, I have to be diligent with it, or I find myself being easily distracted and at the end of the day, wishing I had stayed more organized and focused. Whatever your situation is, it is important to make the best of the time you do have.

SUCCESS

When I teach magazine writing workshops, the first thing I have participants do is write out their personal definition of success. It's that point where you can stop and say, "I did it!" For a stay-at-home dad of three children it might be to publish a parenting article in a national magazine. But for a woman who works twenty-five hours per week and has more time to devote to writing, her goal might be to make ten thousand dollars per year off writing. These are very different definitions, but one isn't better than the other. They are based on what would make each person feel like they made it as a magazine writer.

Although money can be part of your definition, it doesn't have to be. Maybe you are passionate about a cause, so publishing articles on the subject to raise awareness would make you feel successful, and the amount you get paid for the pieces is secondary. On the other hand, it's fine to say that in order to feel successful, you want to make _____ dollars each year.

Your turn. Take some time for yourself and think about what would make you feel like a successful magazine writer. Write down some thoughts or maybe journal about it, but seriously think about it. Then write your definition below or in a journal.

MY DEFINITION OF SUCCESS:

_____

_____

_____

_____

BENEFITS OF GOAL SETTING

BY PAM FARONE

Pam Farone, founder of Careerfulness, a coaching and training company dedicated to helping individuals and organizations find their happy workplace, explains the benefits of goal setting. She says the research favors goal setting, and studies have shown that people will achieve thirty percent more by setting a goal than if they don't.

First: Setting goals can clarify your vision, which saves you time in the long run.

If you are willing to go through a process of really thinking about what you desire, where your passion, strengths, and talents lie, you can move forward in a more productive way. Jumping into a project without thinking it through can lead to wasteful outcomes. Part of goal setting should be thinking about the kind of writer you want to be. Think about where you see yourself. What has been calling to you? When you take the time to think deeply about your vision and desires, then you can step back and set a goal.

Second: Setting goals can take the overwhelm out of the task.

Sometimes the task at hand just seems too overwhelming. The process of goal setting forces us to take something big and break it into manageable chunks. If we just focus on getting to the Emerald City and how far it will take to get there, we'll never take the first step. Goal setting forces us to look at the steps toward getting to the goal. Once that is mapped out, we just need to get to the next milestone. Oz is not as far when we approach it this way.

Third: Setting goals will keep you motivated.

When you get in touch with what you want to create and feel that sense of drive and determination as you think about the endgame, you are more apt to act. Visualizing the outcome and creating steps that make it seem feasible can inspire you to do things you wouldn't normally do. Keeping the goal visible and working on it daily will keep you motivated and more likely to achieve your goal.

As mentioned, goal setting forces us to outline the steps toward a goal. As we achieve each milestone, we gain momentum and confidence. That propels us to keep going.

Fourth: Setting goals will keep you focused.

The world is a very distracting place. There are so many opportunities to get off track and meander, surf, explore, and wander on to the next exciting thing. Setting a goal will help declutter your brain and streamline your efforts. You won't have time to mess around when you've set deadlines and measurable, time-specific tasks. The temptation to flounder is great when we don't know where we are headed. Goal setting will help keep you on pace. Little by little, step by step, focused actions lead to results. Try it!

SETTING GOALS

Now that you have your definition of success identified, it's time to create goals to help you achieve that. Goals are like a GPS for our brain. They provide direction and something to work toward. When we don't set goals, we can feel lost and frustrated, which could lead to not getting anything done. It would be like you getting in your car because you want to go somewhere, but not having any destination in mind. You would end up driving around wasting time. You might eventually find a place to visit, but it would take longer than if you had known where you wanted to go before you got in the car.

Our brains are the same. When we don't give our thoughts something to focus on, they wander aimlessly through the depths of our minds, taking lots of unnecessary detours and turns. Goals give our thoughts direction and purpose.

To make goal setting easier and more effective, create a road map to the final destination.

- Write your goals down.
- Be specific and positive.
- Set deadlines for achieving your goals.
- Be as detailed as possible.
- Say what you will or intend to do.
- Read them each day/post them.

First, start with one or two big goals. Think back to your success definition, and create goals that will get you closer to that.

Using the stay-at-home dad with three kids who wants to have an article published in a national parenting magazine as an example, he might start with regional parenting publications. He has identified two such magazines, and his big goal is to get five assignments in these. He understands he needs more writing experience before he approaches national magazines, and because of his time constraints, this feels like a good place to start.

The woman who defined success as making ten thousand dollars per year from her writing needs to take a different approach. Her focus is going to be more on finding publications with a higher pay rate. She is new to writing for magazines, so she understands she isn't going to make ten thousand dollars her first year and that she will have to work her way up to that. Plus she has a part-time job where she works twenty-five hours each week.

Once these big goals are in place, it's time to break them down into monthly goals related to the big goal, then create action steps for each. This will increase your likelihood of success.

For the stay-at-home dad who wants to publish parenting articles, his monthly goals will focus on finding publications and creating ideas.

The woman's goals will be different. She needs to find paying markets while building her writing experience and credentials.

Once all of these goals are in place, it is time for some action. Providing your GPS the location of where you want to go is great, but you will never get there if you don't press on the gas and start moving. Writing is no different. You must create the steps needed to reach your goals, then give them fuel. The more specific your action steps, the easier they will be.

Another essential element to maintaining and achieving your goals is to reward yourself. Too often we forget to celebrate the small successes along the way, and this can lead to burnout. By adding a simple incentive, you are more likely to stay the course and make it to the end. The rewards don't have to be big or cost a lot of money, they just need to be something meaningful to you. That could be watching your favorite movie, getting an ice cream cone, or going to breakfast with your writing buddy. It doesn't matter what it is as long as it is something you look forward to getting once you achieve your goal.

Following the criteria listed above, here is what that would look like for the dad and the woman.

	STAY-AT-HOME DAD	WOMAN WHO WORKS PART TIME
BIG GOAL	Publish article in national parenting magazine.	Make $10,000 per year from writing.
ANNUAL GOAL #1	I will get three assignments in the *North County Parent Magazine* by June 15.	I will make $3,000 from articles by December 20.
ANNUAL GOAL #2	I will get two assignments in the *Mountain Parents Magazine* by December 15.	I will send out at least 40 queries (approximately 1 per week) with the goal of getting at least one new assignment per month.
ANNUAL GOAL #3	*Because of his time constraints, he is only creating two annual goals for himself.	Get at least 12 assignments from publications that pay at least 20 cents per word.
MONTHLY GOAL #1	Study the two target publications.	Create a list of 10 publications that pay 20 cents per word or better.
MONTHLY GOAL #2	Create a list of 10 ideas for potential queries.	Study *Highroads* magazine and create a list of 5 ideas (a publication she enjoys and it has a decent pay rate).
MONTHLY GOAL #3	N/A	Write and send off 3 queries (including *Highroads*).
ACTION STEP #1	Block out 3 hours total this month to read past issues of the magazines.	Block out two separate 90-minute blocks of time this month to research markets and create a list.
ACTION STEP #2	Block out a 2-hour block of time to create the list of ideas.	Schedule a two-hour block of time to go to the coffeeshop and read past issues of *Highroads* online.
ACTION STEP #3	N/A	Schedule two 90-minute blocks of time toward the end of the month to write and send out queries.
REWARD	Enjoy an afternoon to myself, fishing.	Arrange to go see a movie with a friend.

Now it's your turn. Go back to your definition of success and create your goals based on that. Dream big, but be realistic based on your writing experience and the time you have available to devote to this new venture. Create a big goal, write it down on a note card, and post it in a place where you will see it every day. Next write your annual goals on a note card, and post it in a place where you will see it every day. On separate note cards, write down each monthly goal and below it, the action steps you plan to take to achieve it. Put the reward at the bottom.

REACHING YOUR GOALS

Clear goals are a key to reaching success, but they're not usually enough on their own. Here are some other techniques to help ensure your success.

Visualize

In his book *The Success Principles* Jack Canfield talks about the importance of visualization to achieve your goals. He says visualization activates the creative powers of your subconscious mind, focuses your brain by programming it to notice available resources—that were always there but previously unnoticed—and attracts to you the people, resources, and opportunities you need to achieve your goals.

"When you give your brain specific, colorful, and vividly compelling pictures to manifest—it will seek out and capture all the information necessary to bring that picture into reality for you. If you give it pictures of a beautiful home, an adoring spouse, an exciting career, and exotic vacations, it will go to work on achieving those. By contrast, if you are constantly giving it negative, fearful, and anxious pictures—guess what?—it will achieve those too."

The process of visualization is pretty simple. Close your eyes and imagine your goals as if you have already achieved them. Make the images as clear as possible. If one of your goals is to be published in *National Geographic Traveler*, visualize what your article looks like in the magazine. How does it feel to see your piece in there? I bet it is exciting. Enjoy this scene before pausing and moving on to your next goal.

"Set aside time each and every day," says Canfield, "to visualize every one of your goals as already complete. This is the most vital thing you can do to make your dreams come true."

Share

Find a writing buddy, someone reliable whom you trust to provide you encouragement and support, but who will also hold you accountable—and you need to do the same for that person.

When writing this book, I had a writing partner. I had known him for years and would help him with his novels. When I got this book contract, I knew it would be a big undertaking, and I needed help to get through it. He was more than happy to help and promised to hold me to the fire when necessary. I sent him my schedule and the dates I needed each chapter completed. Then I had until midnight each Saturday to get that week's chapter to him. He did quick check-ins with me during the week to see how I was doing and to encourage me.

I learned early on that when Saturday came, he was all business. He wanted and expected the chapter and made sure I knew it. On one Saturday I was dragging. My chapter was almost complete, but I didn't feel like working on it anymore and I had a friend coming over. I texted him to let him know he would have it on Sunday. That's when the questions started. He wanted to know what I was doing instead of writing. He asked how long it was going to take to finish. He asked why this was more important than honoring my deadline, and when he finally stopped the barrage, I said he would have the chapter by the end of the day. So after my friend left, I put in the couple hours needed to finish it and e-mailed it to him. As tired as I was, I did feel better knowing I stuck to my deadline, and I let him know how much I appreciated his holding me to my schedule.

always nice to have a friend who wants you to succeed as much as you do.

Article Example: Profile

KWAME ALEXANDER, SAYING YES TO SUCCESS![1]

Kwame Alexander's 23-year journey to the 2015 Newbery Medal award for his book *The Crossover* was filled with many ups and downs. But his willingness to say *yes* to potential opportunities and take control over his own destiny enabled his success.

Growing up, Alexander was surrounded by books. His father was a publisher and his mother, an English teacher. Despite his parents' influences, by middle school, he fell out of love with reading, and his passion for books fell dormant.

"I grew up with a man who had written 16 books, gotten his Ph.D. from Columbia University, forced me to read the encyclopedia and the dictionary, made me read books from the time I could walk. By the time I was twelve, I knew *Pedagogy of the Oppressed* by Paulo Freire, I knew the *The Three Musketeers*; I knew literature but I hated it."

When he went to college at Virginia Tech he wanted nothing to do with literature, so he became a biochemistry major with the hopes of becoming a doctor. But during his sophomore year his life took a new direction down a familiar path. He enrolled in a poetry class taught by professor and award-winning poet Nikki Giovanni.

"Taking Nikki's class woke me up and reminded me of the joy and what can happen when you read a poem that knocks you off your feet. It was also at a time when I was meeting a lot of girls on campus. I may not know how to talk to them, but I can certainly write them a poem. Those two things conspired together and I was off to the races."

---

1 Originally published in *2015 Children's Writer's & Illustrator's Market*

He changed his major to English, immersing himself back into the world of literature. During his junior year, he started down the road to becoming a writer and saying *yes* to new opportunities.

In addition to writing love poems to the ladies (one of those now being his wife), he wrote a play. He wanted to produce it, but needed a venue and an audience. After learning about a student leadership conference that was being held at the College of William and Mary, he called the organizer to ask if she was interested in having entertainment during the event. She agreed on the terms, which included payment, and the play was performed for about eight-hundred students.

Alexander said, "After the play, during the Q&A, one of the students asked, 'Is your play going on tour?' [pause] *Yes!* Of course, it's going on tour. At the end of that night, I had bookings for eight colleges, including Rutgers, Princeton, Temple, Hampton University, and so forth. I am a junior in college, and I am understanding what this idea of saying yes means; of walking through a door and figuring out what is on the other side and figuring out how to make it happen."

He continued with his writing, including another play, trying his hand at novels, his poetry and staying open to new opportunities. If someone asked him, "Kwame, have you ever thought about …?" and even if he hadn't, he would say yes. This led him to writing a children's show for television, reciting poetry to a church congregation in L.A. and successfully selling his children's book *Acoustic Rooster and his Barnyard Band* at farmers markets.

If opportunities he hoped for didn't pan out, he didn't let that stop him. When his books were rejected by publishers, he self-published; when he wasn't invited to book festivals, he organized his own; and when he applied for a three-month writing fellowship in Brazil and was turned down, he created his own and invited eight accomplished authors to join him for three weeks in Tuscany.

"There will be opportunities in life we don't get," he said, "and we are going to feel sad and disappointed. But even when people are telling us no, we can say yes to ourselves."

And that is exactly what he kept doing. At an event in NYC, an editor suggested he write a novel in verse for middle school boys about basketball. After seventeen books and twenty plus years of writing, he went to his office (at Panera Bread) and began working on this project. He felt it was the best thing he had ever written. He submitted the manuscript three times to the same agent who had suggested the idea, and she turned him down each time.

After sending it out and getting rejected by twenty different publishers, he decided he was going to publish it himself. But before he could start that process, he got one more response. An editor at Houghton Mifflin said she would be honored to publish *The Crossover*. The book was released in March of 2014. On February 2, 2015, Alexander received the call that it won the Newbery Medal.

"For 23 years of my writing career, I was a jet plane on a runway. With each book and each year, I picked up speed. When I won the Newbery, the plane took off. And it soared 30,000 feet and I haven't come down since. I don't know if I will ever get used to it. Sometimes I wake up and laugh and pinch myself. There is a new normal now."

Winning the award has provided him more opportunities to reach students and publish the books that are important to him.

"I want to save the world. I believe that words can do that, that books can do that. I believe the mind of an adult begins in the imagination of a child. And so, I want to create the most well-rounded, informed, honest, empathetic, connected imagination for children that I can. So that when they become adults, they have truly become more human."

Alexander proves persistence and openness can lead to reaching your dreams. He believes writers should always be prepared to walk through the door because a yes will be there somewhere. It might not be in the way originally anticipated, but it will come.

Alexander has noticed most writers are more than willing to put in the work to be successful at a job for an employer, but when it comes to putting in the work for themselves, it becomes more challenging and difficult.

"If you want to take destiny into your own hands, I think you have to treat your dream like you would a job. You have to put in work for it, and you have to be consistent, and you have to be unwavering in your commitment to it."

He says a good support system is important. Make sure the people around you are going to be encouraging and supportive and at least as smart, if not smarter than you. Surround yourself with other business-minded people who are going to propel you forward.

During a keynote address to writers, he shared, "I was the guy who self-published poetry. I was the guy who was told time and time again, poetry doesn't sell. I was the guy who went to farmers markets. I was you—I am you.

"The only difference between you and me is that I just happened to win this medal thing, and I got lucky. You don't get lucky unless you put yourself in a situation to get lucky. I mean, I think I wrote a good book, but we all write good books. This idea of saying *yes*—it works."

His best advice: "Do it! Tap into your life as a child. Remember what you went through. Pull from those experiences. Write about things that you want to write. Don't try to write to the audience. Remember what it was like to be the audience, and write something you think is real and authentic and beautiful and compelling. I say do it."

CELEBRATE SUCCESSES

FREELANCE WRITERS SHARE THEIR SUCCESS STORIES

JORDAN ROSENFELD: My favorite successes are always finding a home for stories that were rejected elsewhere, and for more money. I was rejected by a big-name publication last year, which hurt my pride. I was able to break that idea into two ideas, sold them to another pub I write for, for almost three times the money the big name pub would have offered. And then about six months later, I cracked the big-name pub anyway with a different piece. My proudest "wins" though, are writing for *The New York Times* and *Scientific American.*

DANIELLE BRAFF: For me, success in freelancing simply comes with scoring assignments. When I first started nearly nine years ago, I could go weeks without writing. Now I could fill my mornings, afternoons, and nights with stories. That's success in my book.

MEGAN HILL: I've written for a local magazine in my hometown of Seattle since I first started freelancing, about eight years ago. I've been a reliable contributing writer, always meeting my deadlines and turning in great content. In fact, over the years, I've been one of the only writers to stick with the magazine through editor changes and other growing pains. The magazine's owner has noticed this and has consistently given me more responsibilities, and I'm now getting paid to manage the magazine's social media channels and act as the managing editor.

TOM KEER: I can think of many successes that range from any of the awards I've been fortunate to win or magazines that have asked me to serve not just as a writer but also as an editor. Or to launch magazines from the ground up, some being print and others being digital. But if I had to pick one success it would be overhearing conversations about my work, held by readers I don't know. I hear what they enjoyed, what they did not, and in that spirit of discussion I know that I've reached my audience. When that group's conversation gets heated I know I've really accomplished my goal. Heated discussion means I've struck a nerve and accessed their heart. No tears in the writer, no tears in the reader. It's sort of like being a third-person omniscient narrator while being in my own skin. It's a trip.

ROXANNE HAWN: When I got the opportunity to write for the Sunday Styles section of *The New York Times*, I was nervous about calling the editor the first time. So I called my editor at *The Denver Post*, and she gave me a pep talk. She told me because of where I live I have a unique perspective he couldn't get from anyone in New York City. She told me that he needed me more than I needed him. I wrote out a little script because I can be too *me* when I get nervous, and I dialed. He answered right away. I introduced myself and asked how he'd like me to send story ideas. He told me, and the whole conversation lasted maybe ninety seconds.

STACEY MCKENNA: I wrote a few pieces on various social justice and public health aspects of drug use and homelessness last fall and winter. During interviews, especially in Denver, some activists were hesitant to talk with me. This last summer, one of those very individuals read a different article I wrote and wrote to me to say how impressed she was. She felt I'd gotten the issues and perspectives right and presented them well. She even compared me to a couple of public scholars whose work I really admire. It was such an honor to have someone on the ground read what I wrote and find it useful. That and other articles like it have had so much more reach than anything I wrote as an academic.

DEBBIE HANSON: I believe that success in the freelance writing world is often shaped by consistent projects and relationships. That said, one of my favorite successes was being given the opportunity to blog on a weekly basis for TakeMeFishing.org. Through my posts, I've been able to share my voice and hopefully encourage more people to try recreational fishing.

MICKEY GOODMAN: A friend had just landed a job in our new mayor's office, and three of us were celebrating at dinner. She began talking about a study they were doing on sexual exploitation and trafficking in Atlanta. I literally dropped my fork. Sex trafficking underage girls? In *Atlanta*, the buckle of the Bible

Belt? I knew immediately it was a major story and queried *Atlanta* magazine, the city's premier monthly. The editor was intrigued, and I began my research in earnest, talking to the D.A., the mayor, juvenile court judges, advocates, and seven young girls living in a safe house. It became a major story and was picked up by CNN, where I was interviewed several times on TV and radio. I also wrote follow-up stories for Reuters that were read around the world, and several other articles. All resulted in first-place awards for the publications.

AMANDA CASTLEMAN: I'd won a Lowell Thomas—travel writing's ersatz Pulitzer—for a scuba feature, something that hadn't occurred in a decade, I'm told. But I still couldn't even get a rejection from one of the big dive magazines. Finally, a contributor took pity and referred me: *Bam.* Suddenly, I was reporting in the Pacific for five weeks, writing a ten-page cover story among other projects. It emerged that an editor's romantic shenanigans had flooded the office with unqualified female freelancers. I'd been tarred with the same brush until a stand-up colleague put in a good word.

This sordid setback taught me a few crucial things. One, keep trying. Two, accept help. And three, rejection—it's not all about you. Don't self-select: Keep pitching unless an outlet specifically says, "You're not a good fit. Shoo!"

CHAPTER EIGHT

• • •

PRODUCTIVITY, ORGANIZATION, AND CREATIVITY

An important element of writing is to understand your personal rhythms. When are you most creative? How much time do you spend mulling over a new idea? What tends to get in the way of achieving your goals?

Sage Cohen, author of *The Productive Writer* and *Fierce on the Page,* says you need to become the expert of your own productivity by studying and trying different strategies and approaches to discover what works for you. Then repeat those things that work and continue to modify and experiment with things that don't.

"You need to know what you are striving for," says Cohen. "What are you trying to accomplish? Why does it matter to you? What has been in your way? Pay attention to your process. Along the way, find practices that keep you connected with the *why*, which is your core purpose or passion. When we stay in that zone, anything is possible. When we are in service to this passion and purpose we have, it is our best way to maximize our ability to be successful."

For author Laura Pritchett, the most important part of the process for her is to understand the balance between her creative and critical brain. "My creative brain helps me come up with ideas and explore issues. Then my critical brain steps in and says you have to shape it and form it and think of your audience. The two war sometimes. Creative brain is saying, I want to write about this. Then the critical brain says, that's stupid, where will you publish it, what will your mother think? What I have learned to do is love and respect them both and give them each a certain amount of time. So the morning goes to my creative brain. That is when I am most dreamy. That's a really good time for me to generate ideas, write personal essays, or explore issues I want to write about. And the afternoon is best for getting out my material to shape it, hone it, tighten it, think of the audience, up the theme, find a metaphor. But I can't start the day off that way."

Like Laura, my most creative time is in the morning, so I block out a big chunk of time each weekday to write. I have found that from about noon to one-thirty, I am not productive at all. I have started taking a break during this time, then I save the afternoon for working with clients, e-mails, and my business tasks.

The key is to find what works for you. Windy Lynn Harris, author of *Writing & Selling Short Stories & Personal Essays*, says she has to trick herself into a productive creative writing session. "It's easy to tweet and answer e-mails, research magazines, and submit work, so of course I gravitate to those tasks the minute I reach my desk each day. Creating new prose is much more intimidating. Harder, too. What works for me: I schedule one-hour blocks of creative writing time during the day. One in the early morning right after the dog gets a walk, another one around ten A.M., then a final session at two P.M. The small investment of time keeps things from feeling too overwhelming while the number of sessions per day guarantees forward movement. I often keep writing once I hit the hour mark, but I don't feel guilty if I switch gears and hop on Facebook."

If you work full time, you will have to experiment and be even more creative. That could be getting up an hour earlier in the morning or staying up an hour after your kids go to bed. Maybe it is cutting television out three nights a week. I've known writers who use their time each day on public transportation to work on their writing. Try out different times and you will soon learn when you can be most productive, even with small bits of time.

5 TIPS ON HOW TO STAY BUSY
AS A FREELANCE WRITER

1. Build your relationships with editors. Be personable, yet professional, in your interactions, and be reliable. Send your assignments on time and to the specifications requested. By doing this, it will make the process easier because you know the editor will respond to your e-mails, and some of the formalities of earlier communications can be dropped.

2. Send another query after you complete an assignment. Once you get an assignment with a publication that you want to continue writing for, keep sending targeted queries. You want to keep that top-of-mind awareness.

3. Always send queries—even when you're busy. It's all in the numbers. The more queries you send, the more assignments you will get. To stay busy as a freelance writer, you need to continually have queries out for consideration.

4. Diversify. Don't rely on one publication and one editor for assignments. Find a few different publications and editors to work with. If an editor leaves a publication, you will be starting over with the new editor and sometimes that doesn't work out.

5. Stay organized and focused by creating goals for yourself, tracking your submissions, and creating a writing space where you enjoy working.

ARTICLE EXAMPLE: Q&A

HOW TO BE A MORE PRODUCTIVE
AND HEALTHY WRITER

Interview with author, motivational speaker, and founder of Writing and Wellness, Colleen Story

For twenty years Colleen Story has worked in the creative writing industry. Specializing in health writing, she has written thousands of articles for publications like *HealthLine* and *Women's Health*. Her expertise and experience have enabled her to work with high-profile clients like Gerber baby products and Kellogg's, and ghost-write books on back pain, nutrition, and cancer recovery. In addition, she is an award-winning author of two novels, *Loreena's Gift* and *Rise of the Sidenah*. She finds her most rewarding opportunities as a motivational speaker and workshop leader, where she helps writers remove mental and emotional blocks and tap into their unique creative powers. She is the founder of Writing and Wellness, a motivational site for writers, and author of the nonfiction book *Overwhelmed Writer Rescue*.

I assume creating a productive writing life is not a one-size-fits-all venture. People have different learning styles and personalities. What are the first few steps writers need to take to identify what will work best for them?

There are several things we can all do to become more productive. We can eliminate distractions, for example, get enough sleep, eat well, complete our most important and difficult tasks first, eliminate time thieves, learn how to motivate ourselves, and a number of other things I talk about in my book on the subject.

But in addition to that, we are all different, and we have to figure out our unique strengths and weaknesses when it comes to getting things done. What do you need to do to get into the flow of writing, for instance? Are you someone who responds to quiet music, or do you need complete silence? What motivates you to go after your goals? Do you need to write them down, create a visual collage of where you want to be five years from now, or compete with a friend to help keep you accountable?

What about your daily schedule? When should you block out time to write? In our society we're led to believe that everyone is most productive from nine to five. But many of us have natural circadian rhythms that favor evenings over mornings. On top of that, we may perform better going from task to task rather than having to jump to another activity simply because of the time on the clock.

A 2014 study by researchers Avnet and Sellier, for example, found that adhering to the clock as much as we do in our culture today can make people less productive and creative than simply allowing them to work on a task until they're ready to move on.

There are a number of other ways that we differ from each other. What kind of exercise best energizes you? For some, it's running; for others, it's walking or biking or yoga. What kinds of foods get you going, and what kinds drag you down? A small piece of chocolate may work for you, but if I eat chocolate, I may crave more and end up eating too much, then all I'll want to do is sleep. Not good for productivity!

We have all these quirks, if you will, that we have to discover about ourselves, and it takes time. I would say the first two things writers need to do is a) become more self-aware, and b) give themselves permission to be exactly who they are. First we have to tune in to our bodies, minds, and spirits to figure out what works for us, for only when we do that can we really start to hear that core inner voice that is so unique. When we are too focused on doing what we think we're supposed to do, or what others tell us to do, that inner voice is drowned out, and it affects not only our productivity but our creativity as well.

Then we have to allow ourselves to create our own unique routines and ignore what anyone else says about them. If you work best typing on an old Remington while wearing a fedora and drinking a nice hot cup of chocolate pu-erh tea at three o'clock in the morning, then by all means, do that, or get as close to that as you can in your life right now.

In relation to productivity, where do you find that most writers struggle? What can they do to fix this?

In today's world, I've found that distraction is by far the biggest factor interfering with writing productivity. Writers talk about it all the time: how they get on Twitter or Facebook and *zap!*, an hour's gone, and they didn't get their writing done. But it's not just social media, though of course that's a big part of it. We can take our work home with us now, and we do. We spend our evenings responding to e-mails and texts when we should reserve these activities for work hours.

Attention is the number-one commodity in our world today. We're bombarded by all kinds of things vying for our attention on our televisions, computers, tablets, and phones, and we're all too willing to succumb to temptation. After all, so many of those things are fun and exciting. But if an advertiser, entertainment company, or even a YouTube star has your attention, he's won. That means we have to battle for our own attention. We have to fight to be sure we place it where we want it. We have to make a conscious effort between nine and ten (or whenever we've determined our writing time will be) to shut everything else off and focus on writing alone.

The other part of the problem is that we've become so conditioned to distraction, we no longer know how to focus. Many of us are addicted to our gadgets, and we feel the consequences when we try to concentrate on something. After ten minutes we become restless and decide we will check just once, real quick. If we're not careful, we end up spending five minutes or more answering that text or that e-mail or responding to that Tweet, and suddenly we've interrupted our flow of thoughts on the story. If not social media, it's a friend or family member who distracts us, or we decide to research something in the story, or we get up to put the laundry in the dryer or whatever. We allow our attention to stray. Once we do, studies say it takes at least fifteen minutes to get that concentration back.

It's not worth it. We don't have the time to waste. We have to train ourselves to stay put and focus. First, remove the temptations as much as you can. Put the phone out of reach, shut off the e-mail and Internet, or use one of the apps available out there that blocks your access. Shut the door, put up the *do not disturb* sign, and leave all other chores for later. Then make yourself sit for your scheduled time. Set a timer if you want to. The good news is that it gets easier the more you practice, but you can't cheat. If you do, you set yourself back to square one.

We have to win the battle against distraction. It kills productivity.

If a writer has limited time to set aside for writing, what advice do you have for her so she will feel successful?

Sometimes life gets in the way and you just don't have time to write. Maybe a family member is ill, or you're working two jobs to get through a financial crisis, or something else is going on that severely limits your time to write. In that case, reduce your expectations. Find fifteen minutes in your schedule and give it back to yourself. We can all find fifteen minutes, no matter what. Then the trick is to dive quickly into the work. Put on the headphones and sink into the story. Allow yourself to write badly. Use the time to practice rather than write a *real* story. In other words, do whatever you must to *produce words* during those fifteen minutes. Don't use it to think about writing, Tweet about writing, read about writing, edit your writing, etc. Use it to actually write. That way, you'll see progress in terms of pages accumulating, which will motivate you to continue until your life eases up and you can expand your writing time.

If you're not in this type of situation, however—where your life is kind of falling apart—and you still think you have very limited time to write, I would suggest re-evaluating your priorities. How important is writing to you? Maybe it's not that important, and that's okay. If it *is* important though, you may need to think about giving something else up to make room for it. Writing requires your commitment.

What do writers need to keep in mind when creating a writing schedule for themselves?

When creating a writing schedule for themselves, writers need to keep in mind two things: They must honor their own unique makeup, and they must remain open and flexible.

First you need to tap into your own high-energy times. When do you have the most creative energy for your work? Try to schedule your writing time then. Maybe that's first thing in the morning, before you leave for work or before the kids get up, or maybe it's after work, for thirty minutes in the car, before you drive home. Try to avoid low-energy times, as that's when your willpower is weakest, and you're likely to blow it off.

Next stay open and flexible. If that writing time you set doesn't work for a day or two, keep trying it for at least a week. But if after a week you're not getting anything done, don't be afraid to experiment with another time. I typically change my writing schedule three or four times a year. I may write first thing in the morning for a few months, then switch to the evening hours just after dinner. I may write in the morning and edit at night, or vice versa. Schedules change, life changes, and we need to be ready to change with it to stay productive. Work with a schedule as long as it works, then go back to the drawing board if you need to.

How are productivity and wellness connected?

How much writing do you get done when you have a headache, when you're tired, or when you're filled with self-doubt? How productive are you when you're depressed or feel like your writing doesn't matter?

Our physical, mental, and emotional wellness has *everything* to do with how productive we are. Researchers are figuring that out now. There are studies showing how sleep deprivation destroys productivity; how stress eradicates creativity; how fatty, fried foods dumb us down; and how self-doubt poisons our dreams.

When we're happy with what we're doing, have a strong sense of purpose, feel confident, and possess the energy of good health, we always get a lot more done. It seems like common sense, and it is, but it's amazing how often we neglect this simple relationship. Bottom line: The better you feel, the more productive you will be.

In relationship to productivity and wellness, if writers could implement only one strategy into their writing life to improve wellness (which in turn will help with productivity), what should that be?

If I were to recommend just one thing for writers to do regularly that would significantly boost their wellness and their productivity, in turn, I would say *exercise* with several annoying exclamation points. I've been a health writer for twenty years, and I've studied reams of research journals, and if there's one single activity that stands out for helping you to not only enjoy better health and age more slowly, but have more energy, reduce stress, and keep your brain sharp, it's exercise. It does all those things and more.

People say, "I'm too tired to work out." Usually you're too tired because you haven't exercised. It's just the way the body works. The more you move, the more energy you have, and the better your brain functions. Studies show that people become more creative when they're walking, for example, simply because they're moving and getting the blood flowing to the brain. If you want more energy and you want your brain to be sharp and ready to write, make sure you're getting in at least thirty minutes of some type of exercise every day.

Anything else you want to add?

There's one more thing that's key for productivity, and that's motivation. You have to be sufficiently motivated to get stuff done. If you don't really want to do it, or you just can't get up the energy for it, it's probably because you're not motivated enough. We've all heard stories of people who managed to write and complete great works of art despite all sorts of obstacles, simply because they were sufficiently motivated to do so.

If you're having trouble with this, you may want to spend some time to find out why. Try freewriting on the statement, "I'm just not motivated to write right now because …," and see what your answer tells you. Then you can use that information to fix the problem.

REJECTIONS

Rejection. We hear this word all the time in the writing world. It is such a harsh word. It is definite, direct, and always seen as negative. Rejection, or the fear of it, can be a real threat to motivation and productivity. When I think of rejection, I think of someone being left at the altar, a child being ignored by her parents, or a guy asking a girl to dance and she laughs in his face. That *to me* is rejection.

Yet I see writers throw the word around like a ball and even wear it as a badge of honor.

I want to know when a *no thank you* from an editor, agent, or publisher became synonymous with rejection. I don't see them as the same thing at all.

Imagine you are at a nice restaurant and the waiter asks if you are interested in ordering the chef's special: chicken breast stuffed with blanched fresh spinach leaves and Boursin cheese, sautéed shiitake mushrooms, and baked asparagus with balsamic butter sauce. You think it sounds good, but you planned on getting salmon, so you say, "No thank you."

When the waiter goes in the kitchen to put the order in and the chef finds out you ordered something besides her special, do you think she screams and drops to her knees, sobbing, wondering what she did wrong, and agonizing over the fact that you didn't want what she was offering?

I don't think so. It boils down to the fact that you were offered something you didn't want, so you responded politely with a "no thank you." It wasn't anything personal. You just didn't feel like eating chicken.

Isn't that the same thing that happens in publishing? We send queries out and editors respond with a *yes* or a *no thank you*. They are not rejecting us or saying our work is bad, they are simply responding to us. They know what they want, and not everyone is going to offer them what they are looking for. Rejection can beat us down, but a response is just that—a response. There is no judgment attached to it, making it easy to move on. It is much easier to say, "I got a response from an editor today ..."

So once you start sending queries out, you are going to get "no thank yous." It is all part of the business. To be successful with magazine writing, you need to be thankful you received a response and move on; figure out another market to send the query.

ORGANIZE YOUR WRITING

Creating good organizational tools for your writing will enable you to be more productive and successful. Play around with different systems until you settle on the ones that work better for you. Then stick to those and make slight adjustments as necessary. The more organized you are, the more time you will have for writing.

TRACK SUBMISSIONS

Keeping track of everything you send out is going to help you stay organized. It doesn't have to be complicated, but it does need to be done. When I first started writing for magazines I had a red spiral notebook where I tracked everything I sent out. I wrote down the date, what I sent, whom I sent it to, then made notes when I received responses. Now I use a Google Drive spreadsheet. This allows me to sort the information in different ways if I am looking for something. I can also see pretty quickly if I am meeting my goals with the number of queries I am sending out and get a quick overview of how many queries turned into assignments.

Here is an example of what my system looks like.

ARTICLE IDEA	TYPE	PUBLICATION	SENT TO:	E-MAIL ADDRESS	DATE	RESPONSE	FOLLOW UP	PAYMENT
5 GUYS LIVING THE DREAM	query	*Success*	Jane Doe	j.doe@gmail.com	11/21/2016			
5 HEALTHY IDEAS FOR YOUR KID'S LUNCH	FOB	*Family Circle*	Dan Smith	dsmith@fc.com	11/6/2016		11/21/2016	
DURANGO, CO	query	*Sunset*	Tim Hill	Hill@sun.com	10/20/2016	Yes!		$350
ROUNDUP: 10 BEST RESTAURANTS ALONG ROUTE 66	query	*AAA Highroads*	Nicole Port	port@aaa.com	10/3/2016	Yes!		$600

The spreadsheet works for me. I have a freelance writing friend who uses the app Trello to track her submissions, and that works for her. Regardless of how you track your submissions, the important thing is that you create a system to track everything you send out.

GETTING RID OF DISTRACTIONS

Freedom
Blocks apps and websites on your computer and phone for a designated amount of time to improve your focus and productivity.
https://freedom.to

Cold Turkey
Temporarily blocks distractions so you can focus and be more productive.
https://getcoldturkey.com

SelfControl (for Mac)
Temporarily blocks distractions so you can focus and be more productive.
https://selfcontrolapp.com

Write or Die
Aims to eliminate writer's block by providing consequences for procrastination and rewards for accomplishment.
https://writeordie.com

PRODUCTIVITY TOOLS

Toggl
   A tool to help you track your time and discover how you are using your time.
   https://toggl.com

Remember the Milk
   A smart to-do list app for busy people.
   www.rememberthemilk.com

Wunderlist
   A program/app to organize your to-do list.
   www.wunderlist.com

ORGANIZE YOUR WRITING SPACE

Article Example: Feature

FENG SHUI FOR WRITERS, CREATING A SPACE YOU LOVE

Originally appeared in Wow! Women on Writing September 2010
www.wow-womenonwriting.com

Feng shui, the ancient Chinese art of placement, dates back to before the Bronze Age, but the techniques and philosophies behind it still work today. Considered an art and science, feng shui goes beyond decorating a space to make it look good; it is meant to create harmony in your surroundings and ultimately in your life.

It wasn't until the late twentieth century that feng shui found its way across the ocean to land here in the West. In the book *Feng Shui With What You Have,* authors Connie Spruill and Sylvia Watson say, "Even though Feng Shui has changed throughout the ages, traveling from East to West, the basic premise remains as relevant today as it was in ancient times: Use nature as a guide to create environments where you feel balanced, inspired, and nurtured."

As writers, it is important to have a space that allows the words to flow and feng shui can help accomplish that. The good news is that it doesn't have to cost a lot and can be done with items you already have in your home. This article will share simple ways you can implement feng shui into your writing space, making it a place that encourages creativity, inspiration, and success.

When looking at your own writing space, one of the first things all the experts believe you should do is get rid of the clutter, all those extra things you have lying around that don't serve a purpose. By doing this you open up the *chi*, the invisible life force or energy that is in and around our bodies and our environment. We experience *chi* through our five senses, what we see, hear, feel, smell, and taste. Too much clutter stops the flow of *chi* and can make us feel stuck and stressed.

Once you declutter you can begin creating a writing space that works for you. If you are a piler, give yourself lots of horizontal space, and if you are a filer, have lots of vertical space. Terah Kathryn Collins, founder of the Western School of Feng Shui, points out that having a feng shui-friendly space is not about being immaculate, it is about having a space that doesn't irritate, confuse, or overwhelm you.

Spruill and Watson also add that you should have appropriate lighting, an ergonomically comfortable chair and a window or picture that provides you with a depth of view that you can turn to to exercise your eyes regularly.

When positioning your desk, you should not have your back to the door. If there is no way to avoid this, then add a mirror so you can see the entrance.

You also want your space to be unique to you. Collins says, "Writers are intuitive, creative people who work from the inside out. Setting up your writing space should be no different—you should do it from the inside out."

She encourages writers to set up their room first, personalizing the space with art, photographs, and objects that are meaningful and inspire creativity. Then step back and examine the feng shui of the space. Does it flow? Does it have too much or too little of an element? Does anything need to be moved?

At this point you can even use a bagua map to help focus attention on the areas that correspond with your goals in life (self/career, wisdom/knowledge, future/fame …). The room is divided into eight sections. The bagua is a template that can help you determine where those areas are in your writing room and how to enhance each one with a variety of objects, colors, and scents.

You will also want to keep in mind the yin/yang energy in your writing space. The concept of yin/yang or opposites is an important aspect of feng shui: light/dark, male/female, loud/soft. Together, these complementary forces make a whole and one cannot exist without the other. Spruill and Watson describe yin energy as dark, quiet, still, and small and yang energy as light, with sound, active, and big. When you have a good balance between both of these, the environment will feel comfortable and harmonious.

Drawing on aromatherapy and the sense of smell when we write can be a powerful tool. Spruill and Watson recommend using rosemary for recall and memory, jasmine or any citrus for alertness and productivity. Keep in mind that aromatherapy use depends on the culture and background of the person.

Other Enhancements You Can Use in Your Office

• Have a vase full of yellow and some bright orange flowers. The orange can help with connectivity to new plots while the yellow, based on intensity, can promote investigation, and the brighter the yellow the more clarity.

• Bring in a water element like fountain or flowing-water sound effects (very lightly in background) as wood, the creator, cannot survive without water for nourishment.

• Electronics that use a sudden boost of energy to run (printer, fax machine, copier) can be draining to us. Don't have this type of equipment too close to your creative workspace. Plants can be used to minimize the effects of the electromagnetic fields.

• Hang a wooden chime in your window. The movement activates stagnant *chi* and stimulates your money-making potential. Wood is the symbol of growth.

• Electronics like your computer generate electromagnetic fields that can reach as far as thirty inches. Once again, you can use plants to minimize the effects.

• Boost the south wall of your office for fame and recognition. Place articles sold, awards you have won, diplomas, pictures, or letters from famous people on your south wall.

The five elements, fire, water, wood, earth, and metal, give us the tangible aspects of feng shui. Each is unique and has specific colors, textures, shapes, and objects associated with it that will bring out the essence of each one. Fire and water are seen as catalysts, and wood, earth, and metal are content elements. Although each is used for a different purpose, it is important to remember that how these elements are combined and interact with each other is what makes a space feel welcoming or forbidding.

EARTH
COLORS: brown, yellow, beige, peach
SHAPE: square
MATERIALS: brick, stone, ceramic
OBJECTS: pottery, tile, rocks, sand, plaid fabric, masonry, marble

FIRE
COLORS: red, orange
SHAPE: triangle
MATERIAL: electricity
OBJECTS: lamps, candles, animal prints, computer, fireplace, artwork with the color red or depicting pyramids, obelisks, spires

Dr. Jill Bolte Taylor, author of *My Stroke of Insight*, writes in front of a fireplace in the winter or in her sunroom when it is warmer. She incorporates the elements of fire and wood depending on the season. "I have a great view of the outdoors—woods. I enjoy the natural quietness of these spaces. For me an effective space is a quiet place where I find peace ... no demands on my time, minimal distractions, and natural comfort."

WATER

COLORS: black, dark blue

SHAPE: wavy

MATERIAL: glass

OBJECTS: water features, aquarium, fabric with wavy patterns, mirrors, artwork depicting a water scene

Karen Quinn, author of *Testing for Kindergarten* and *The Ivy Chronicles* has an office in her apartment. A key element in her environment is water.

"I love being in this space because I'm surrounded by things I love—paintings I've made myself, books, my favorite oriental rug, a view of the ocean, and my two cats are always sitting at my feet."

WOOD

COLORS: green, blue

SHAPE: rectangle

MATERIALS: wood, paper

OBJECTS: plants, wood items, books, fabric with stripes, silk, artwork depicting landscapes, plants, or flowers

Sandra Dallas, author of *Whiter Than Snow, Prayers For Sale* and *Tallgrass,* converted a covered porch into a private space overlooking her backyard. She incorporates many wood elements in her space from the view to the books. "I love—Indian rugs, folk art, floor-to-ceiling bookshelves, a rolltop desk, an antique pie safe that holds files, my awards. When I'm writing, I usually prop up antique pictures of people who look like my characters or odds and ends that I plan to include in the book."

METAL

COLORS: white, gray, silver

SHAPE: round

MATERIAL: metal

OBJECTS: metal items, coins, metallic finishes, fabric with circles or metal sheens, rounded arches

Laura Resau, author of *Red Glass* and other middle-grade novels, has her "sweet little fifties' rig," a ten-foot aluminum trailer parked in her driveway, that she uses as her office. The whole structure is metal, but Resau has done a great job incorporating all the elements on the inside of her writing space.

"It's filled with things that are meaningful or inspiring to me—photos and pictures and quotes hanging on the walls, a string of lights, pillows, special rocks, and candles on the table where I write."

The Tao, an Eastern philosophy, states that everything is connected and in order to be happy we must live in harmony with nature, our surroundings, and the people around us. By making adjustments to our physical environment, we can get rid of unnecessary obstacles in our way and clear our pathway toward writing, success, and happiness.

Sources used for this article:

Connie Spruill and Sylvia Watson, *Feng Shui With What You Have*, 2004

Skye Alexander, *10-Minute Feng Shui*, 2002

Western School of Feng Shui, www.westernschooloffengshui.com

CREATIVITY

Whether you are writing an in-depth, research-heavy service piece or a light travel essay, creativity is at the heart of it. When you nurture this side of yourself and allow it to show in your writing, the more it will resonate with readers. Here is a piece I wrote for *The Writer* that explains how to cultivate creativity to enhance your writing.

Article Example: Feature

TAPPING INTO YOUR CREATIVITY

Creativity is at the core of everything we do as writers. Without it, our protagonists would lead mundane lives, articles would be boring lists of facts and poetry wouldn't exist. Creativity is the fuel we need to breathe life into our writing and to the worlds and characters we create.

So if creativity is a key to writing success, are there ways to enhance and cultivate this part of us? Mihaly Csikszentmihalyi, psychology professor, leading expert in the field of creativity and author of *Flow: Living at the Peak of Your Abilities* and *Creativity: Flow and the Psychology of Discovery and Invention*, believes there are. After years of studying creative individuals in different fields from science to the arts, he found ways we can all access our creativity more consistently.

As with any creative venture, writing takes time and success does not happen overnight. Csikszentmihalyi reminds us, "A generally creative accomplishment is almost never the result of a sudden insight, a lightbulb flashing on in the dark, but comes after years of hard work."

There are common characteristics among successful creative people. First they understand the rules of the field. To be a writer means learning grammar and proper writing techniques. To become a successfully published author, a writer also needs to learn the rules and procedures for publishing. We can't show up at a publisher's doorstep, hand him our manuscript, and expect him to read it and publish it. There are steps in place that need to be followed.

Next creatives are passionate about their work, yet extremely objective about it as well. A good writer can pour herself into her writing, but then step back, evaluate it and revise it to create the best work possible.

The ability to enjoy the process for its own sake is another characteristic among this crowd. Writers who function at this creative level love to write because they find great joy and satisfaction in the process. It doesn't mean they don't want to be published, but the need to express themselves with their writing is first and foremost.

Laura Resau, author of *Red Glass* and other middle-grade novels, understands this. "If I go more than a couple days without writing, I get really grumpy and cranky. I can't really take a break from writing."

THE CREATIVE PROCESS

While researching creativity, Csikszentmihalyi found definite components to the creative process. Writers typically move back and forth between different parts of the process.

PREPARATION

During this stage writers need to keep their eyes open, curiosity awakened, and a notebook handy. This is a time to gather ideas and experience new adventures. Andrew McCarthy, travel writer and author of *The Longest Way Home*, takes this to heart when he is out on assignment in a new city. "Sometimes I take copious notes; other days pass with barely writing anything. I try to write details of things I see, quotes and feelings. Facts I can get later, once the dust settles."

Here are a few ideas to try:
• Jot down thoughts about your experiences.
• Save interesting stories and headlines from the newspaper.
• Keep brochures and information from places you visit.

INCUBATION

During this phase, bits and pieces from the preparation phase percolate in our minds. Ideas come together, stories begin to form, characters appear, and plots unfold.

There are creative tools to help facilitate these ideas:
• Idea maps
• General plot sketches
• Character sketches

- Collecting photographs and images of characters and settings (Pinterest is a great one for this)

INSIGHT
This is the aha! moment when everything begins to come together. We get excited about our idea and want to take it further.

EVALUATION
This can be the most emotionally trying part of the process, when we feel uncertain and insecure. We wonder if the idea is original enough and worth pursuing. We think about who the audience will be and question if we have the ability to make it happen.

ELABORATION
This is when we must write the novel, article, poem, or short story. To see it complete, we have to make the time and persevere until the project is finished.

GETTING PAST OBSTACLES
Most of us encounter obstacles in our writing life. Distractions get in the way, we are too tired to write, or we can't organize all the thoughts in our head. There are strategies to move past these to become a more productive writer.

FIND YOUR INNER CHILD
Children are naturally curious; they delight in the strange and the unknown. The more we can adopt that same curiosity in our everyday lives, the more it will help us as writers. By keeping an open mind and being a keen observer of the world, there is never a shortage of ideas.

DEVELOP HABITS OF STRENGTH
After creative energy is awakened, it must be protected. When asked in an e-mail what writers can do to connect to their creativity instead of all the electronic devices, Csikszentmihalyi said, "We

must avoid distractions and escape outside temptations and interruptions. If we do not, the concentration will break down and we will default to our old behaviors. If you want to avoid distractions, then take steps to avoid it. Don't feel that you have to have your cell phone with you all the time, don't look at your e-mail except once or twice a day, silence your gadgets. After all, they are there to help you, not to mess with your brain. Some people will think you are a Neanderthal for living off the grid, but hey, so what?"

TAKE CHARGE OF YOUR SCHEDULE

To be a productive writer, writing time needs to be a priority and put into our schedule. We must honor this time and not look at it as something that can be disregarded. This may mean setting boundaries with friends and family and letting them know that our writing time is nonnegotiable.

MAKE TIME FOR REFLECTION AND RELAXATION

It is important to have some downtime to recharge but also to let new ideas or aspects of current projects incubate and roll around in our minds. Set aside or schedule this time. This reflection time can happen while sitting quietly or while doing a favorite activity like gardening, woodworking, or baking.

SHAPE YOUR SPACE

Your writing space should inspire you. In an article I wrote a few years ago about feng shui for writers, Terah Kathryn Collins, founder of the Western School of Feng Shui, shared that a productive area is not about being immaculate, it is about having a space that doesn't irritate, confuse, or overwhelm you. Collins said, "Writers are intuitive, creative people who work from the inside out. Setting up your writing space should be no different—you should do it from the inside out." Personalize it with art, photographs, and objects that are meaningful and inspire creativity.

DO MORE OF WHAT YOU LOVE

If you want writing to be a part of your life, examine your current habits and lifestyle and see if there is a way to increase the things you love to do (writing) and let go of, hire out, or delegate those aspects of your life you dislike.

"It is much easier to be personally creative when you maximize optimal experiences in everyday life," wrote Csikszentmihalyi.

And by doing this, you can consciously create the writing life you always dreamed about.

FREELANCERS LOOK BACK

ONE THING THEY WISH THEY HAD KNOWN EARLY IN THEIR CAREERS

JORDAN ROSENFELD: Don't be afraid to nudge and try again. I used to give up too easily. Now I'm dogged and scrappy in my persistence.

DANIELLE BRAFF: That I shouldn't put up with difficult editors. The great thing about being a freelancer is that if you don't like your boss, you can just find a new one.

MEGAN HILL: I wish I would have hired a business coach earlier on in my career. Working as a lone wolf is difficult; having a professional business coach on retainer to bounce ideas off works great. I wish I had done it sooner.

TOM KEER: To think of myself just as a writer. Most folks try to put creatives in a slot. You're a newspaperman or a food writer or travel writer or a novelist. I have written across so many different genres that I can't really say I'm one or the other. I'm a writer, and if you're a writer, you can write anything. If you're unfamiliar with a style or format, learn about it. Study it. Own it. After all, that's precisely what keeps us alive.

ROXANNE HAWN: The people you know right now may only provide work leads for your first year of freelancing, so you need to keep building your network and not get complacent.

STACEY MCKENNA: I'm still pretty early in my career and constantly learning, but I've had several editors, especially lately, say they're really happy to get on the phone with new-to-them writers before and during an assignment to help with voice and vision.

DEBBIE HANSON: That it's important to have a high degree of patience when starting out. Don't expect a freelance writing career to take off overnight. It takes time to build credibility and editorial contacts.

MICKEY GOODMAN: It's a hard way to make a real living—particularly in the beginning. I was happily married to a husband who could support us until my writing took off. In the meantime, I taught creative writing to seventh graders, became assistant to the president of a major commercial real estate corporation, and became a stay-at-home mom. But I never stopped writing. Occasionally I'd sell a story or two and developed a following writing about the joys and pitfalls of parenting for a local paper. Advice: Get a day job, but continue plying your craft.

AMANDA CASTLEMAN: As a paper-trained journalist, I had an inherent mistrust of PR and marketing people. But they often provide vital sources and timely angles for travel writers, especially given magazine lead times of three to thirty-six months. I also wish I'd sought more help from books, workshops, conferences, and writers' groups, instead of reinventing the wheel. Freelance success doesn't hinge on talent alone: You need contacts, constantly refined skills, and the ability to run a business. Stand on the shoulders of the giants who came before you!

CHAPTER NINE

HOW TO WRITE AND SELL PERSONAL ESSAYS

Life. We are given one to use however we want. Everyone's life is different, yet there are elements of our lives that connect us to others, that remind us we are all human. It doesn't have to be a shared experience for that connection to happen. When we hear about a tragedy happening in the world, we may not be anywhere near the incident, yet we feel sad or angry. Or we watch a video of someone reaching out to help a complete stranger, and tears well in our eyes.

As humans, we have a need to connect and relate to one another. Personal essays bridge that gap between our experiences and those who read our words. Personal essays give us the opportunity to share a part of ourselves and let others know they are not alone. They can also help us navigate our days and provide us perspective.

Personal essays are one of my favorite types of writing. They allow me to process situations and events in my life. I use essays to reflect on my past, and they give me a voice when I feel silenced.

In the world of magazine writing, personal essays are a great way to break into a publication. If you recall, back in chapter two I shared an idea that came from a real-life experience about the best way to keep spending at a minimum for kids' birthday parties. The idea became a personal essay that shared this dilemma and how we solved it. It was written in first-person narrative form and published in *FamilyFun*.

Essays are approached and written differently than a typical article. Because of their personal nature, you don't have to write a query letter first. You include a cover letter explaining why you feel your essay is a good fit for the magazine, where it fits in the magazine, and a little about yourself. Then you include this with your essay and send it off.

Editors prefer this approach rather than a query with personal essays because it is easier for them to understand the style and tone of your essay in its full form. After all it is based on something that you experienced; therefore, only you can write about it. With articles, topics can be written in a variety of ways by any number of writers. This is not the case with essays. So rather than waste time, most magazines want a cover letter with your piece.

E-Mail Cover Letter Example:

Dear Ms. Stephen,

Enclosed below is my 795-word essay "The Threads That Bind" for your consideration. It revolves around my son's attachment to his blanket, but in a broader sense looks at how we all have items that bring us comfort. I believe it is a good fit for your "Family Moments" section.

Thank you for considering "The Threads That Bind."

Sincerely,
Janet Smith
(include contact information here)

WHAT IS A PERSONAL ESSAY?

A personal essay is just that—it's personal. As the authors, we are exposing a truth about ourselves, a revelation, or an epiphany. We are reaching out to readers, hoping that our experiences resonate with them. A good essay is not about shining a spotlight on the writer and saying, "Look at me." It is about shining a light on an issue, an idea, a memory, or a thought.

For award-winning author, essayist, writing coach, and instructor Laura Pritchett, personal essays go beyond that. One of her favorite quotes is "If no one knows you, then you are no one," from Dan Chaon. For her, personal essays make us *someone* to one another, fellow human beings on Earth, trying to live right.

"On the spectrum of keeping things private and being public I veer toward making your inner life public," says Pritchett. "Not because I feel like I am a navel gazer or narcissist. But because books and essays and writing are what made me less lonely and helped me to understand how to live in the world when I was growing up. I don't think it was modeled to me in my household how to be very human, how to listen and be a friend. It was more of a survival situation. It was a very rough childhood, and I turned to writing to teach me what to do when someone tells you bad news or how to be more empathetic, more human. ... Writing has taught me how to live. And if I have anything to say about my personal life that might help someone, then it's worth it."

A personal essay is more than just an anecdote that explains an experience. It goes deeper. Whether it is a heartfelt piece about a tragic event that makes us cry or a humorous situation that exposes a common problem, making us laugh out loud, an essay sheds light on the topic. It takes a close, honest look and finds a way to reach out and connect with others.

Dinty W. Moore, in his book *Crafting the Personal Essay*, explains, "The personal essayist (that would be you) takes a topic—virtually any topic under the big yellow sun—and holds it up to the bright light, turning it this way and that, upside and down, studying every perspective, fault, and reflection, in an artful attempt to perceive something fresh and significant. But it is always an effort, a trial, not a lecture or diatribe. ... The best writing also provokes an emotional reaction, be it laughter, sadness, joy, or indignation. Keep in mind, though, that there exists a vast difference between those thoughts, ideas, and memories that elicit a powerful reaction from you, the writer, and those that will have the desired impact on someone who does not know you or have a stake in your well-being."

Importance of Story

A good essay has all the components of a story. There should be a good beginning, middle, and end. Use the tools of fiction, dialogue, setting, and the five senses. Then all these components need to support one theme. As with any good story, you need to draw readers in at the beginning, making the subject clear, and establish the tone. Well-done essays are based on emotion and experience.

For most magazines that publish personal essays, the word count is typically under one thousand words. Skip the lengthy buildup. You need to jump right in.

Moore says, "An essay needs a lighted sign right up front telling the reader where they are going. Otherwise, the reader will be distracted and nervous at each stop along the way, unsure of the destination, not at all able to enjoy the ride."

As with fiction, dialogue can help create the scene and present a clear picture of two or more characters. Here is one I wrote for an essay book I self-published that took a lighthearted look at family. It gives the reader insight into my relationship with my husband and my feelings about Donny and Marie. The title is "Bucket List."

My husband strolled into my home office and handed me an envelope. "Here, happy early birthday."

"Really?" I love surprises and this definitely counted as one for two reasons. One, my birthday was still a few weeks away, and two, birthdays are not usually high on his priority list. I often wondered if they were even stored in his memory at all.

I opened the envelope, took out the papers, and unfolded the group of them. My eyes skimmed the page then stopped. Las Vegas.

"We're going to Vegas?" I stood up from my chair.

He grinned, "Yes, we are going to Vegas."

I wrapped my arms around him. "Thank you! When are we leaving? Where are we staying? How long are we there for?"

"Keep reading."

I let go of him. "Okay. Okay," My hands trembled and my face hurt from smiling. I found the dates, the hotel, and then went to the next page. I gasped, looked at him, then looked back down at the page. "Is this for real?"

"Yes." He let out a small laugh.

I stared at him, "You got us tickets to see Donny and Marie?"

"Yes."

I let out a scream. "We are going to see Donny and Marie? Oh my God. Really?" I jumped up and down. "This is going to be the best birthday ever!" I gave him another hug. Looked back at the paper. Gave him another hug and sat back down. I exhaled. I was going to see Donny and Marie.

This duo had been part of my life since I was eight years old. Their television variety show had captured my attention every week. I wasn't sure if I was a little bit country or a little bit rock and roll, but it didn't matter. I watched each week and colored in my Donny and Marie coloring book. The week Donny was on *The Love Boat* I cleared my busy elementary school calendar to make sure I was home to watch it and I wasn't disappointed.

Weaving in the five senses can also ground your reader in the scene. Here is an example of setting the scene from an essay I shared in an earlier chapter. My goal was to paint the picture of fishing in the middle of winter and why I was there.

As I stood in the Cache la Poudre river and looked around, I realized I was the only one crazy enough to be out fishing in December. My chest waders kept me dry, but I still felt the freezing temperature of the water seep through to my skin. The sounds of the trickling water calmed my breathing, and I lifted my fly line out of the river, gently cast it back and forth a few times before placing it back on the water. Like an addict, I needed a hit, but mine involved a fish biting the fly at the end of my line.

I could have opened with *I stood in the river in the middle of December hoping to catch a fish*. It still has the same basic meaning, but it does nothing to ground the reader in the scene.

One of the most important aspects of a personal essay is your willingness to be honest and open. Don't hold back from your readers. If you are writing about an experience you want out there in the world, then you have to willing to go all in, to share those thoughts and feelings that may be uncomfortable. If you are hesitant, readers will pick up on that and they will not trust what you are saying.

"The private essay hides the author," says Moore. "The personal essay reveals. And to reveal means to let us see what is truly there, warts and all."

You can't do this if you are worried about what your family and friends are going to think of it. It will paralyze you. For Windy Lynn Harris, author of *Writing & Selling Short Stories & Personal Essays*, the personal essay and the memoir have much in common including the writer's responsibility to tell the truth without slandering anyone in the process. "That's a fairly straightforward mission," she says, "but it doesn't address those times when the truth doesn't meet the definition of slander. When the story tells a truth that would embarrass someone else or hurt their feelings. For instance, writing about the time your mom called you fat. Or that time your brother was arrested during your high school play. Or that time you cheated on your first husband. Your responsibility in these cases is to acknowledge that other people are affected by your publishing success. Period. That might mean you warn your brother that you've been writing about him or maybe soften your mom to the idea that you've written about the fights you used to have, but you are in no way obligated to leave out details or scrap a piece of writing. If you think one of your essays might cause harm to a relationship, be sure you're willing to risk that before sending it out to the world."

Revelation

Regardless of the length of your essay, there has to be a lesson learned, a revelation, or a realization. Pritchett is a writing instructor, and this is an area where she finds students miss the mark, and she has to give what she calls, her "dream killer speech."

"No one cares about your awesome fishing trip—maybe your kids do, but no one really cares. But the reason they will care is because on that fishing trip you realized or you felt something or you came to an epiphany on something that matters to the rest of us."

Looking back to my story about fishing, it is more than just an article about me out on the river. It is about me becoming obsessed with my new hobby and that feeling of joy it brought me. The idea that a newfound activity can be so consuming is something many people can relate to. It may not be fishing, it may be knitting or rock climbing or painting, but it is that idea that we find an activity we love doing and we will do anything to make it happen.

Universal Theme

This takes us right into one of the more important components of a personal essay, the universal theme. This is what shifts the essay from a private story for family and friends to one that may resonate with strangers. It's what moves it from a story about ourselves to a story others can relate to.

Beth Levine, in her article "Personal Essays Find Truths in Small Moments," says, "The most effective essay takes a small moment and lets it be a microcosm of a larger truth, a truth that resonates with all, even though this moment is personal to just you. If you don't get that kernel, then what you are writing is merely gossip and even worse, boring."

Pritchett says the more personal it is about you, the less it is about you. The more you reveal about yourself, the more it will resonate with the reader. You have to talk about something that matters to someone other than yourself. To do that you must have a theme, a point. "I always say to myself, what's this about, about. The first about is me dumpster diving with my children. What is it *about*, about? It's about recycling our aluminum and my concern for the environment and how this translates into concern about this one little planet we're on in space."

Pritchett believes we all have core themes and we should all take time to identify them. These are topics and subjects we are drawn to or haunted by. Ones we keep returning to in our journals, our thought processes, our writing: religion or faith or feminism or justice or death. Where does your head keep circling back to? Think about these themes and write them down. Honor those subjects.

One of Pritchett's core themes has always been communication. She had trouble with that as a child because it wasn't modeled for her. Some of her other core themes include love, the natural world and wanting to protect it.

Process

For me, an essay begins with a spark or kernel of an idea. It can come following an event, something I read about or heard, an event that happened, a question I have. ... I never know when one is going to hit. The ones I sit down to write are the ideas that are persistent and shove their way to the front of my mind.

Once the essay is written, it's time to step back. When Pritchett finishes writing one in the truest fashion possible, she puts it away for two weeks. "Then I have what I call the 'come to Jesus moment.' I stare at the essay and ask, *Is that what you really wanted to say?* And, *Are you okay with that going out into the world?* As much as I am advocating to be public, there are some things I have written about and said the most honest truth, but I don't want it out there in public. So then I have to decide if I want to pull back or not publish it."

I have one personal essay I wrote years ago when my son was seven years old. He had a favorite blanket he slept with every night, and it was starting to fall apart. I continually resuscitated it, hoping to give my son more time with his blanket. I liked this idea for an essay, but it didn't have a universal theme. At this point it would be a cute story that my parents might enjoy.

Around this same time, I was talking with a friend. She told me about how her husband felt their five-year-old son was too old for his blanket and took it away from him. She said her son was devastated, and she was struggling with whether this was the right thing to do.

It made me think more about what I should do with my son. Should I take his blanket away? I let it roll around in my mind for a few more days, then sat down to write about it. I wanted to wrestle with the idea and process it for myself.

What I ended up with was an essay that explored the theme of comfort and security. It was first published on Beliefnet.com, then in *Chicken Soup for the Mother and Son Soul*, and finally *Ideals* magazine reached out to me to ask if they could publish it in their special Mother's Day issue.

Here is the essay.

Article Example: Personal Essay

THE THREADS THAT BIND

After enduring a few stitches and a couple of minor surgeries, it was a relief when the most recent operation was successful. My seven-year-old son, Drew, was thrilled. These were always rough times for him, but the older he got, the easier they became. With this last attempt, a few more months, maybe even a year, was added to the life of his favorite blanket.

With a look of sadness and concern in his blue eyes, he approached me one morning last week, holding his blanket like it was a wounded animal. His blond hair was going in all directions, obviously the result of a rough night's sleep.

"Mom," his voice cracked. "There are more holes. Can you fix them?" I looked at the lifeless piece of fabric in his hands. I gently picked it up by the corners to assess the recent damage. There were a few big holes and frayed edges. Being careful not to pull on any of the life-bearing threads, I said to him, "I will see what I can do, Honey."

Like a skilled surgeon I carefully examined the patient. This was not going to be easy, but I came up with a plan. I called Drew over for my prognosis. "Your blanket isn't looking so good. If it is okay with you, I will sew it to some other fabric and patch up the holes. Okay?" He agreed.

The next morning, he reluctantly put his priceless possession into my hands and left for school. I felt I should have had him sign a medical release form before he left, freeing me from all responsibility should something go wrong. (I am not the best at sewing the truth is I am not very good at all.) After an hour of skillful work (luck actually), the surgery was a success. My reward—a big smile showing both of his adorable dimples, a hug, and a "Thank you, Mommy" that oozed with sincerity.

Now some people may say that Drew is getting too old for a blanket and I should just throw it away. Part of me agrees with that, but then the other part of me remembers wrapping him up in that same blanket and rocking him to sleep. This blanket has been more than just a source of comfort at night; it has been a superhero cape, a bandage for wounded stuffed animals, and something to have a pretend picnic on.

Maybe I am using the blanket to hold onto something that is out of my control. My son is growing up and I can't stop that. While I do celebrate each new stage in his life, the truth is I miss holding him in my lap. I miss having him fall asleep with his head resting on my chest, I miss smelling the powdery fragrance that can only be found on a freshly cleaned baby.

Sure, I can tell him he is too old for a blanket and that it is time for him to grow up, but why? Because I am the adult and I decided he didn't need it anymore? If you think about it, adults have favorite "blankets" too—an old nightshirt that's full of holes or a car stranded in the garage that we swear we are going to fix someday. We would never admit that we have a favorite "blanket." We would never want anyone to know that we have things in our lives that provide us comfort and we would have hard time doing without them.

So what will I do when Drew needs me to fix his blanket again? I'm not sure. I will have to cross that bridge when it comes. For now, though, I am going to enjoy the time I spend with him. I am going to share in his joy as he learns how to read. I am going to fill with pride when he tests for his next belt in karate, and I am going to hang up all the wonderful pictures he makes especially for me. He will be seven only once and I want to relish all the exciting moments he will experience at this time in his life.

I kiss him goodnight and tell him to have happy dreams. Quietly I thank God for giving me my son and for helping me realize just how special each day with him is. I slip into my favorite nightshirt with all the holes in it, then grab my favorite quilt and a family photo album. I nestle into my favorite chair and arrange myself until I am at maximum comfort. With a big sigh, I open the album and begin reliving moments of the past seven years, many that include a little boy's favorite blanket.

PERSONAL ESSAY CHECKLIST

____ Does it have a strong opening?
____ Is there a universal theme?
____ Is there a revelation in the essay?
____ Do you have a good story with a beginning, middle, and end?
____ Do you weave in the five senses?
____ Did you proofread your essay for errors?

WHERE TO PUBLISH PERSONAL ESSAYS

There are many places interested in publishing personal essays. As with articles, check the guidelines carefully before submitting your piece.

CONSUMER MAGAZINES: The listings in *Writer's Market* will say if a magazine accepts personal essays.

TRADE MAGAZINES: *Writer's Market* is also a good source for trade publications.

LITERARY MAGAZINES: *The Sun, Narrative,* and *Ruminate* are always looking for well-written essays. *Poets & Writers* is a great resource for finding information about these and other literary publications: https://www.pw.org/literary_magazines.

LITERARY JOURNALS: Many universities publish a literary journal like *Colorado Review, The Missouri Review,* and *Tampa Review*. They accept personal essay submissions. *Poets & Writers* has a list of these as well: www.pw.org/content/literary_journals_us_mfa_programs.

ANTHOLOGIES: The main anthology that comes to mind is *Chicken Soup for the Soul*. They continue to put out a few books each year, so they always need content. www.chickensoup.com

CHAPTER TEN

HOW TO WRITE FOR ONLINE MARKETS

The Internet opens up a whole new arena for magazine writers and provides many different types of writing opportunities. Some are good, others, not so much. But if you are aware of what to look for and how to find the decent paying jobs that allow you to showcase your skills, you can expand your writing options beyond print with these choices.

- Magazine websites
- Online magazines
- Blogs
- Content mills

The process for publishing online is similar to print, but the time-line is usually faster because they are updating their content more frequently. As with print, you have to research the markets, study their content, and find the best fits for what you want to write.

MAGAZINE WEBSITES

Most print magazines have an online counterpart. Many times, there is a different editorial staff for the online version of the magazine because they have their own online-specific content. For instance, if you go online to *Backpacker* and find the contributors guidelines (www.backpacker.com/page/guidelines), you will see links to various posts related to what they are looking for with submissions, including features, queries, and then a section for online-only. They say on their site, "Our main goals here are to create awesome content our readers will love, and drive traffic to the site (so viral = great)." One difference for online content is they are looking for listicles (more about these in chapter three) like "11 Things Every Hiker Should Know About Fitness." These articles will have a photo for each point and two to five sentences about it. *Backpacker* also wants slideshows for their website, definitely something you would not find in print.

Bitch magazine is another one that breaks their guidelines into print magazine guidelines and online writer guidelines. This lets you know exactly what they want for each platform and what to pitch. The good news is you send different ideas to each one, giving you more options for this market.

The procedure for getting an assignment for the online version is usually similar to submitting to the print magazine. Study the online content, come up with ideas, and query. As always, read the guidelines to make sure you submit the way the editors are requesting.

Pay attention to the pay rates. Be aware that the online pay rates might be lower than the rates paid for print articles. They have more content that needs to be put out there. A print magazine typically has to fill one issue per month, whereas the online site may change content weekly or even daily.

ONLINE MAGAZINES

Numerous magazines now are exclusively published online. As with print, read their guidelines carefully and study the publication. Because online content is read differently, there are additional things to keep in mind when you study the articles to better understand the style and tone. First pay attention to the use of hyperlinks. Are there links to sources and/or links to additional information that enhance the content? If so, you may want to make note of sites you intend to link to in your query, and you will need to incorporate links into any articles you write for the publication. Also notice the length of the articles and how they are formatted. Are the paragraphs short? Are there more bullet points and lists? Consider these things when you get ready to query the online magazine.

For a few years I wrote regularly for the online magazine, *WOW! Women on Writing*. Because there are no space limitations online, my word count was more flexible. The editor would ask me to keep it between fifteen hundred and two thousand words. That's a big range and not something I get when writing for print publications. If I referenced a book or author, I included the appropriate links for readers to get more information. With the formatting, I blocked all the paragraphs, which means instead of indenting, I aligned all the text to the left and added an extra blank line between paragraphs.

Some online magazines are interested in more than just the article. They are looking for additional content to enhance the piece. *Condé Nast Traveler* editor Katherine LaGrave encourages writers to think beyond the text. "Let us know in your pitch if you're interested in submitting more than copy. Is there video you'd be able to take? Any photos you can submit? The more you can show your potential story as a dynamic package, the more attractive it is to us."

BLOGS

Writing blog posts for businesses or organizations can be a great way to build up your skills as a writer. Many companies use content marketing to draw potential clients and customers to their site. People are drawn to good content. They don't want to feel like they are being sold something. Because of this, companies are looking for well-written posts that provide helpful information and resources to visitors. They are willing to pay a writer to create that content.

Initially, the pay may not seem that great (fifty to seventy-five dollars per post), but the posts are usually between only three hundred and five hundred words, and if you write them in an hour or two, it's not a bad pay rate.

I have written blog posts for a few different companies over the years including one that helped other businesses with their blogs. This company hired writers like me to write the posts. I didn't get a byline for my writing, but I enjoyed doing it because I learned to write faster and still put out good content. Plus the work was pretty consistent. For another job I was hired to write fun and informative posts geared toward new parents. I was given a byline linked to my website with each post.

If you are considering writing blog posts, take into account how much you are getting paid and how many hours you will have to put in to research and write the posts. You don't want to commit to something where you end up getting ten cents per hour. You can find blogging jobs at freelance writing sites like, www.freelance writing.com or www.fundsforwriters.com. The job platform, Indeed .com also lists these types of opportunities.

CONTENT MILLS

If you start looking on the freelance writing job boards, you are sure to see a listing for content writers with the promise of making twenty-five to forty dollars per hour. As the old saying goes, "If it sounds too good to be true, it probably is." Chances are this writing job is being offered by a content mill. This a company that hires writers to generate large amounts of text designed to attract search engine bots, not necessarily human readers. The purpose of the content is to boost rankings in search engine results and get visitors to click on the advertisements. Well-written or researched content is not a requirement.

In an article for *Ars Technica*, freelance writer Chris Stokel-Walker talks about his experience writing for a content mill for six months. On average, he churned out 4,156 words each day and says he earned enough to buy an Olive Garden main course, dessert, and soft drink.

According to Stokel-Walker, "In journalism, fifteen hundred words of well-crafted, in-depth reporting can take several hours at best. But in the content mills, you must churn stuff out quicker at the expense of quality. Put simply, people aren't really meant to read what you write. Content mills make product to fill a page, creating the impression that something is there. It's the marshmallow fluff of content."

If you have dreams to write for magazines and you want to build up your skills, writing for these types of markets is not going to help you. Stay away from jobs where the pay is based on page views and page clicks, places that say writing experience not necessary, jobs where you are asked to focus more on SEO (search engine optimization) and keywords more than good writing, and ones that ask you to turn out a lot of content in a short amount of time. Writing for small regional publications where you might get fifty dollars for an article is a much better use of your time than turning out poorly written content.

FINAL ONLINE ARTICLE CHECKLIST

____ Does it have an intriguing title?
____ Does it have a good lede?
____ Are all hyperlinks functioning and formatted correctly?
____ Did you cover all the information promised in the query?
____ Did you check spelling and punctuation?
____ Is the word count where it needs to be?
____ Did you include a short bio with links to your Web page/ social media sites?
____ Did you include links for sources mentioned?

ADVICE FROM FREELANCERS

JORDAN ROSENFELD: At least seventy-five percent of freelancing these days is online—so don't overlook it. Online markets tend to like shorter content to match attention spans, and need writers who can turn out content fairly quickly since they post more frequently than print mags.

MEGAN HILL: It's always important to be consistent and reliable. You can be a great writer, but that is secondary, in my opinion, to being reliable. Meet your deadlines no matter what.

TOM KEER: Online can be tricky. A few hacks:
1. Make sure you and your editor are simpatico in the scope of the work to be completed.
2. SEO (search engine optimization) writing can ruin your craft by dumbing down your writing. It's like playing a sport with someone who is worse than you. You'll need to allow a bit more time to artfully create sentences and paragraphs that hit the SEO mark, but do it in your own style and with your own voice.
3. Watch the compensation. It's difficult to make a living at twenty-five dollars for 2,500 words.
4. Use digital as a way to test out markets that might be of interest to you.
5. Remember the Web's reach. So write something you're proud of for that day.
6. Remember the Web's archival potential. Writing a heated op-ed will be around when your grandkids are reading digital material. You might regret those words later on, so pick topics carefully.

ROXANNE HAWN: Honestly I treat online markets the same as I do print ones (what few I still have). You need to think about how people read things online versus in print (much more skimming and scanning), but the research and writing are similar. You may just have to structure the piece a little differently.

STACEY MCKENNA: Watch your contract rights and seriously consider how they'll fit into your bigger picture. Some websites are much greedier than print when it comes to this, and if you aren't careful about it, the restrictions could make it impossible to sell related pieces to multiple outlets, which is so important for actually making a living.

DEBBIE HANSON: Learn as much as you can about SEO (search engine optimization) writing techniques. Find out what key words and information the online audience is searching for, then try to fill that need.

CHAPTER ELEVEN

USE MAGAZINE WRITING TO BUILD YOUR AUTHOR PLATFORM

Author platform is a frequently used term in the publishing industry. Agents, editors, and publishers appreciate when a fiction author has an established platform, and it is a necessity for those who write nonfiction books. Writing for magazines is a great way for authors to build one. Whether you write fiction or nonfiction, having published articles with a byline and a short bio at the end will help you gain exposure.

What is a platform? Think of it as a stage in a theater and you are the one everyone is coming to see. The audience is made up of people you know (friends, family, colleagues) and those you have connected with on social media or through other networking opportunities. Some theaters are small and intimate, others are large.

An effective platform is one where you have a genuine rapport with your audience, and they want to hear what you have to say. Some of these contacts are friends and family, and others are mere acquaintances, but regardless, you have in some way made a genuine connection. Marketing guru Seth Godin calls this building your tribe, a group of people who have a shared interest (you) and way to communicate (social media, e-mail …).

Just because an author has lots of followers on different social media venues doesn't mean he has an effective platform. High numbers don't equate to good connections. An author who has ten thousand followers on Twitter but never interacts with them does not have a good platform. Another author who has only two thousand followers but engages with those followers has a stronger platform. She has a way to reach out and connect to other people.

Godin says, "Marketing used to be about advertising, and advertising is expensive. Today, marketing is about engaging with the tribe and delivering products and services with stories that spread."

Writing magazine articles is a great way to appeal to potential readers and ultimately build your platform. Through the articles you are providing inspiration, information, or entertainment to the reader. If they like what they read, a short bio at the end like "Jane Smith is the author of *The Next Best Novel*" might encourage them to look you up and learn more about you and your book. The article also gives you something to highlight on your website and on social media.

For nonfiction authors this is a fantastic way to position yourself as an expert. Writing articles related to your book topics adds to your credibility and shows people you understand your subject matter. It is a way to establish trust and build your tribe. The bio at the end can provide the title of your book and information on how to reach you. In addition, since many magazines have their articles online, it's a good way to increase your SEO (search engine optimization), making your name show up higher in searches.

I know firsthand that articles reach people. For years my article "How to Find Success in the Magazine World" appeared in the front of the *Writer's Market*. At the end of the article my bio lists my website. I have had numerous writers reach out to me to say how much they enjoyed the article, ask me a quick magazine question, and even a few who wanted to hire me to help them write for magazines. This never would have happened had I not written this article, and all the articles I have written over the years have established my platform enough to get me the contract to write this book.

Regardless of the genre you write, you want to connect with readers. That's why we are writers. We have stories we want to share or information we want to convey. Our writing is pointless without someone on the other end reading our work. Writing and publishing articles opens up the possibilities to reach so many more readers, and unlike social media, it allows people to enjoy your writing and hopefully encourages them to want to read more.

FIND THE THEMES

So how do you begin? This book gives you all the information you need for querying and pitching your ideas. But you may be unsure how it applies if you write fiction. You may think that since you made up the world and story in your book, writing nonfiction articles won't help you, but it will. Like I said earlier, when someone reads and enjoys an article, they are making a connection with the writer. Even though your books are fiction, you still have an impact on the reader.

What can you write about? Even if you write fantasy and have created a whole new world, many topics related to your book will make good articles. Let's work through an example:

Miss You Once Again by Kelly Baugh is a women's novel. Here's the basic premise of the book:

After her nana's death, Lee, an independent young woman from the mountains of Colorado, returns to her childhood haunt in Eden Grove, Mississippi, to single-handedly settle her grandmother's estate. With her nana's ghost guiding her through the minefield of childhood memories, fractured relationships, family history, and sweet tea, Lee is pushed to a crossroads where she must decide whether to stay on her independent journey or take a chance on a different future and fight for the man she loves.

There are many key elements, topics, and themes in the book that can be the basis of great articles. Here are a few:

- Sweet tea
- Summers in Mississippi
- Southern cooking
- Outdoor adventure
- Friendship
- Family
- Colorado
- Gardening
- Loved ones who have passed on

WHO IS YOUR IDEAL READER?

After identifying the themes and overall topics, it is important to narrow these down to your ideal reader. When you are trying to build your author platform, you want to target the right audience. Everyone may enjoy your book, but there should be a certain type of person you are writing for. For *Miss You Once Again* the ideal readers are: Women in their thirties to forties looking for a sweet, charming story (think Hallmark).

REFINE YOUR IDEAS

Next, it's time to break down the big topics into smaller article ideas based on the key elements and topics in the book. For each of the themes, create a separate idea map (chapter two). This tool will help you break down the big concepts into more specific article ideas.

Here are some that will work for *Miss You Once Again*:

Sweet tea

- 10 refreshing sweet tea recipes

- The history of sweet tea
- Sweet tea culture
- Sweet tea with a kick; 5 cocktails to enjoy on a hot summer night

Family

- 5 tips on researching your family history
- Front porch culture and how it binds family and friends
- What everyone needs to know about settling a family member's estate

Gardening

- Folklore behind flowers in Mississippi
- Why gardening relieves stress
- 3 ways to can and preserve cucumbers
- The importance of good soil and how it helps your garden grow

Outdoor adventure

- Interviews with the top four women rock climbers in Colorado
- Three great national parks to experience thrilling adventures
- The best gear for backpacking in the backcountry
- How to keep adventure in your life even after having kids

YOUR TURN

In a journal or on a notecard, write down five key elements/themes/topics from one of your books or works in progress. Now identify your ideal reader. On blank sheets of paper, create idea maps for each of the five concepts you came up with. Write down your favorite idea from each idea map and make a plan to begin pursuing those ideas right away.

If you write nonfiction you will do the same thing. The big difference is you want to focus on topics where you want to be seen as an expert. My friend LeAnn Thieman, an author and professional speaker, applies this idea of using magazine articles to build a platform well. Early in her career when she began building her platform, her target audience was nurses. At that time, she had her memoir, *This Must Be My Brother*, sharing her role in Operation Babylift; and she had co-authored *The New York Times* bestseller *Chicken Soup for the Nurse's Soul*.

Her goal was to reach nurses as a way to promote her books as well as her speaking career. She targeted nurses' magazines and websites, and submitted articles to them on various nursing-related topics.

"With *Chicken Soup for the Nurse's Soul*," she said, "I offered one of the stories to be printed monthly in a major nursing journal, then shared a lesson that each story taught, to support and encourage nurses in their benevolent careers. I received no payment for the article under the condition that my byline would have the title of the book and my contact information. That, along with my speaking and other marketing efforts, resulted in that book hitting *The New York Times* best-sellers list, and then selling one million copies. When I co-authored *Chicken Soup for the Caregiver's Soul*, I shared stories in caregiver magazines, then began writing articles to serve caregivers, such as '12 Tips on Caring for Caregivers,' 'How to Support Caregivers Over the Holidays,' 'What Every Employer Should Know About Caregivers', etc. That book sold nearly one-half-million copies, but more importantly, those articles ministered to the thirty-four million caregivers in America."

Thieman eventually went on to co-author twelve more *Chicken Soup for the Soul* books while becoming a well-known and well-respected speaker. The published articles helped build her author platform and helped her advance her speaking career. She has received numerous speaking engagements from people who contacted her after reading one of her articles. All of this eventually led to her inclusion in the National Speakers Association Speaker Hall of Fame.

Reaching out to and resonating with readers is the goal of any writer. Writing magazine articles can broaden the readership for you and any novels or nonfiction books you have written or plan to write.

GLOSSARY

ANECDOTE—A short story about a particular situation or event.

BYLINE—A line in the article that identifies the writer.

CIRCULATION—The number of magazines a publication prints of each issue.

CLIP—A print or electronic copy of a published article.

CONSUMER MAGAZINE—A magazine intended for the general reading public.

CONTRIBUTOR COPY—A free copy of a publication sent to contributors.

COPYRIGHT—The exclusive legal right to reproduce, publish, sell, or distribute the article.

COVER LETTER—A short letter that accompanies a finished piece of writing.

COVER LINE—Short titles or statements that appear on the cover of a magazine to entice readers to read those articles.

DEADLINE—The date you need to turn your piece in to the editor.

EDITOR—The person responsible for managing the content, layout, and design for a magazine.

FIRST-PERSON ARTICLE—Personal narrative told from a first-person perspective, using *I* or *we*.

FOB (FRONT OF BOOK)—Small, newsy pieces toward the beginning of a magazine.

GALLEYS—Initial proof of an article as it will be seen in the magazine.

HARD COPY—Print copy of a magazine.

INVOICE—Document sent to a magazine requesting payment for an article.

KILL FEE—The amount of money a publication will pay in the event the article doesn't end up running in the magazine.

LEAD TIME—The number of months ahead a magazine is working.

LEDE—The introduction to an article.

MASTHEAD—The page in a magazine listing the staff of the publication.

MEDIA KIT—Detailed information about the magazine and its readership, compiled for advertisers.

NUT GRAPH—A paragraph giving a brief overview of an article. Think "in a nutshell."

ON SPEC—A shortened term for on speculation. It is when you send a completed article to an editor without an official contract, and if they like it they offer you a contract.

PAYMENT ON ACCEPTANCE—Payment for an article is sent to the writer after the editor accepts the piece.

PAYMENT ON PUBLICATION—Payment is sent to the writer after it appears in print or online.

PSEUDONYM—A fictional name used to conceal the identity of the author. Also called a pen name.

PUBLISHER—Manages the business operations of a magazine.

QUERY LETTER—One-page pitch letter to an editor of a magazine.

REPRINT—An article already published that the writer has the rights to sell again somewhere else.

RIGHTS—A type of copyright granted to a publisher.

SAMPLE COPY—A past issue of a print magazine.

SIDEBAR—Additional material related to the content of an article that is usually in a separate box or section alongside the article.

SIMULTANEOUS SUBMISSION—When you send the same query to different publications.

SLANT—A specific angle to an article.

SLUSH PILE—Unsolicited articles sent to the editor of a magazine.

TRADE MAGAZINE—A publication containing news and information related to a specific trade.

WELL—Center of the magazine that contains the feature story.

WORD COUNT—The number of words that make up the article.

WORK FOR HIRE—Work that is commissioned, and the writer does not own the right. Bylines are not always given.

WRITER'S GUIDELINES—Information for writers, provided by the magazine, that explains how and what to send to get an assignment or piece published.

APPENDIX

List of Writing Organizations

Whether you write for magazines full time or part time, being a member of a professional writing organization can help you move your career along. It will help connect you with other freelancers, provide resources, and keep you informed about what is happening in the industry. Some have publishing requirements, others do not.

The list here is comprised of national organizations related to freelance writing. Most states have great writing organizations. They may not be specifically geared toward freelance writers, but it is always helpful to stay connected to your local writing community.

AMERICAN SOCIETY OF JOURNALISTS AND AUTHORS
www.asja.org
Annual Dues
Established: 1948
Publishing requirements to join
Professional organization of independent nonfiction writers.

THE AUTHORS GUILD
www.authorsguild.org
Annual Dues
Established: 1912
Various levels of membership depending on publishing experience
Professional organization for writers dedicated to supporting and protecting the writing life for all working and aspiring writers. The Guild advocates for authors on issues of copyright, fair contracts, free speech, and tax fairness. They offer guidance and services on selling books to agents and publishers, contract advice, and resources for writers.

THE INTERNATIONAL WOMEN'S WRITING GUILD
www.wwg.org
Annual Dues
Established: 1976
Open to all women writers
Community of women writers with diverse backgrounds. Provides professional resources, mentoring, and support.

NATIONAL ASSOCIATION OF INDEPENDENT WRITERS AND EDITORS
www.naiwe.com
Annual Dues
Established: 2007
Open to freelance writers and editors
The primary focus of NAIWE is to provide a simple, ready-to-use website and to support you as you develop the online and marketing components of your career. Their primary goal is to help freelance editors and writers earn a living through writing and editing.

NATIONAL WRITERS UNION
www.nwu.org
Annual Dues
Established: 1981
Various levels of membership depending on writing income
An activist organization of writers who work together to get better wages and conditions for all of us. Members get access to valuable resources (contract advice, press passes, etc.).

List of Writing Conferences

More than one hundred writing conferences are hosted each year in the United States. Some are genre focused like the Romance Writers of America Annual Conference, and others, like the Writer's Digest Annual Conference have a variety of sessions on different genres and aspects of the writing world. They vary in size, specialty, and cost. Think about what you want to get from the conference. Look closely at the selection of workshops, the faculty, networking opportunities, and cost. Consider attending at least one per year that fits your needs and your budget.

At the event keep an open mind and challenge yourself to attend sessions that aren't related to what you are writing. For instance, as a magazine writer you can learn a lot by going to sessions on crafting great dialogue or writing great description. I believe you can always learn at least one useful piece of information in any writing session.

Here is a small list of annual conferences that include freelance writing sessions.

AMERICAN SOCIETY OF JOURNALISTS AND AUTHORS WRITERS CONFERENCE
www.asja.org/2018-ASJA-Annual-Conference
When: May
Where: New York City

BINDERCON
A writing conference and community for women and gender-variant writers
bindercon.com
When: Spring
Where: Los Angeles, New York City

BOOK PASSAGE TRAVEL WRITERS AND PHOTOGRAPHERS CONFERENCE
www.bookpassage.com/travel-writers-photographers-conference
When: August
Where: San Francisco Bay Area

LAJOLLA WRITER'S CONFERENCE
lajollawritersconference.com
When: October
Where: LaJolla, CA

NORTHERN COLORADO WRITERS CONFERENCE
www.northerncoloradowriters.com/conference/2018-ncw
-conference
When: May
Where: Fort Collins, CO

**SHAW GUIDES: GUIDE TO WRITERS CONFERENCES & WRITING
WORKSHOPS**
writing.shawguides.com

WILLAMETTE WRITERS CONFERENCE
willamettewriters.org/wwcon
When: August
Where: Portland

WRITER'S DIGEST ANNUAL CONFERENCE
www.writersdigestconference.com
When: August
Where: New York City

Online Resources to Find Market Information

Free

- All Freelance Writing: www.allfreelancewriting.com
- All You Can Read: www.allyoucanread.com/magazines
- Funds for Writers: www.fundsforwriters.com/markets

Paid

- Mediabistro AvantGuild: www.mediabistro.com/avantguild
- Duotrope: duotrope.com
- Writer's Market online: www.writersmarket.com

Submission Tracker

ARTICLE TITLE	TYPE (QUERY, ESSAY, FOB)	PUBLI- CATION NAME	SENT TO	EMAIL OR ADDRESS	DATE	RESPONSE	FOLLOW UP	DUE DATE	PAY- MENT
Going Rogue	Query	*The Writer Magazine*	Dan Anderson	danderson @fakeemail .com	8/30/2018	Yes		11/1/2018	

Query Template

Dear _____,

Good Hook (1–2 sentences)
• Catch editor's attention

Article Content (2–5 sentences)
• Explanation of what will be in the article
• Show you are familiar with your topic

Specifics (1–2 sentences)
• Estimated word count
• A department, if applicable
• Possible experts you are going to interview

Purpose (1 sentence; can be combined with information in the Specifics section)
• Explain what the reader will get from the piece: "Your reader will be informed/entertained/inspired …"

Qualifications (1–3 sentences)
• Why are you the perfect person to write this piece?
• Publication credits

Call to Action
• One sentence that encourages the editor to take action. "I look forward to talking with you more about this idea."

Closing
• Sincerely, then your name

ARTICLE EXAMPLES INDEX

In chapter three I explained the different types of articles and explained a little about each one. Here are those specific articles providing you with an example of each while also giving you more helpful writing information.

CONTRIBUTORS

DANIELLE BRAFF: Freelance Writer and Editor

Danielle Braff is a full-time Chicago-based freelancer. She is a frequent contributor to the *Chicago Tribune* and *Crain's Chicago Business*, and her writing has also appeared in nearly every national magazine. Her clips can be viewed at www.daniellebraff.com.

AMANDA CASTLEMAN: Writer, Photographer, Instructor

Amanda Castleman has contributed articles and photography to *AFAR, Outside, Islands, BBC Travel, Delta Sky, Robb Report, Bon Appétit,* and the *International Herald Tribune* among many others. She's also worked on thirty-odd books including titles for *National Geographic, Frommer's,* and Rough Guides. A renowned journalism instructor since 2003, she still teaches an annual Travel Writing Master Class online and a week-long spring workshop in Rome. www.amandacastleman.com

DIANE J. COHEN, ESQ.: Diane graduated Rutgers Law School (New Jersey) in May 1982 and was admitted to practice in Colorado, Massachusetts, and New Jersey. Her experience is diverse. She has served as a civil attorney, criminal defense attorney, and prosecutor (assistant district attorney, Middlesex County, Massachusetts). Currently she practices on a part-time basis including pro bono and volunteer with the Larimer County Bar Association on the Committee for Free Legal Clinic for Veterans and as a volunteer attorney at the clinics.

PAM FARONE: Founder of Careerfulness, a coaching and training company dedicated to helping individuals and organizations find their happy workplace, Pam combines her 20-plus years in HR with her coaching and improv background to create a transformative experience for her clients. www.careerfulness.com

MICKEY GOODMAN: Content Creator, Ghostwriter, Memoirist, Journalist

Mickey Goodman has written more than 700 bylined articles for scores of publications including Reuters International, the *Huffington Post*, *People*, *This Old House*, *Veranda*, *Southern Living*, Womansday.com, Countryliving.com, and others. She has ghostwritten three books. *Nine Lives of a Marriage—A Curious Journey* is available on Amazon.com. The latest two will be published in 2017. www.mickeygoodman.com

DEBBIE HANSON: Freelance Writer

Debbie Hanson is a freelance writer living in Fort Myers, Florida. Her work, which focuses on freshwater and saltwater fishing, has been featured in publications such as *Florida Game & Fish* magazine, *USA Today Hunt & Fish*, *BoatU.S.* magazine, and *Times of the Islands* magazine. You can read her weekly blog posts at TakeMe Fishing.org and visit her personal blog at Shefishes2.com.

WINDY LYNN HARRIS: Windy is the author of *Writing & Selling Short Stories & Personal Essays: The Essential Guide to Getting Your Work Published* and the founder of Market Coaching for Creative Writers, a mentoring program. She's a prolific writer, a trusted mentor, and a frequent speaker at literary events. Her long list of short stories and personal essays has been published in literary, trade, and women's magazines across the United States and Canada, in places like *The Literary Review*, *The Sunlight Press*, and *Literary Mama*, among many other journals. Learn more about Windy at her website: www .windylynnharris.com.

ROXANNE HAWN: Writer, Journalist, Author

A traditional journalist based in the Rocky Mountains of Colorado, Roxanne Hawn worked as a staff writer and editor for ten years before ditching it all to freelance. She never looked back.

MEGAN HILL: Freelance Writer

Megan Hill is a freelance writer based in Seattle. She writes about food, travel, and the outdoors for a number of local and national publications, both online and in print.

TOM KEER: Award-Winning Freelance Writer and Editor

He lives with his wife, two kids, and four English setters in Wellfleet, Massachusetts. www.thekeergroup.com, www.tomkeer.com, tom@thekeergroup.com

STACEY MCKENNA: Freelance Writer

Based in Fort Collins, Colorado, journalist Stacey McKenna is an unapologetic generalist and tangent chaser. She covers anything that captures her attention, but mostly travel, adventure, nature, and social science. She writes for both print and online publications including *Aeon*, *iExplore*, *Narratively*, and *Horse Illustrated*.

JORDAN ROSENFELD: Freelance Journalist, Author of Seven Books

Jordan is author of *Writing the Intimate Character* and three other Writer's Digest Books. She has been published in *The Atlantic*, *GOOD* magazine, *Mental Floss*, *New York* magazine, *The New York Times*, *Salon*, *The Washington Post*, *Writer's Digest* magazine and many more. Follow her: jordanrosenfeld.net

COLLEEN M. STORY: She is on a mission to inspire people from all walks of life to overcome modern-day challenges and find creative fulfillment. Her latest release, *Overwhelmed Writer Rescue*, is full of practical, personalized solutions to help writers and other creative artists escape the tyranny of the to-do list and nurture the genius within.

With more than twenty years as a professional in the creative industry, Colleen has authored thousands of articles for publications like *HealthLine* and *Women's Health*; worked with high-profile clients like Gerber baby products and Kellogg's; and ghostwritten books on back pain, nutrition, and cancer recovery. Her literary novel, *Loreena's Gift*, was an Idaho Author Awards first-place winner, New Apple Solo Medalist winner, and *Foreword Reviews* INDIES Book of the Year Awards winner, among others.

Colleen frequently serves as a workshop leader and motivational speaker where she helps attendees remove mental and emotional blocks and tap into their unique creative powers. Find more at her motivational site, Writingandwellness.com, and on her author website (colleenmstory.com), or follow her on Twitter.

Editors

KASEY CORDELL: Features editor with *5280* magazine, a city magazine in Denver, Colorado, featuring local issues, dining, arts, entertainment, and living well in the Mile High City.

5280's name derives from Denver's elevation of 5,280 feet above sea level. It is published monthly.

ROBBIN GOULD: Editor with *Family Motor Coaching*, a monthly member magazine providing news concerning motorhome technology, the RV industry, and the association.

TOD JONES: Managing editor with *The Costco Connection*, the monthly magazine published for the members of Costco Wholesale and for others curious about the world of Costco.

KATHERINE LAGRAVE: Senior digital editor with *Condé Nast Traveler*, a luxury and lifestyle travel magazine published by Condé Nast.

TYLER MOSS: Editor-in-chief with *Writer's Digest*, a national magazine for professional and aspirational writers that has celebrated the "Writing Life" since 1920.

JONAH OGLES: Articles editor with *Outside*.

Since 1977 the mission of *Outside* magazine is to inspire participation in the world outside through award-winning coverage of the sports, people, places, adventures, discoveries, environmental issues, health and fitness, gear and apparel, style and culture that define the active lifestyle.

MICHELLE THEALL: Editor for *Alaska* magazine.

Founded as the *Alaska Sportsman* in 1935 (renamed *Alaska* in 1969), *Alaska* brings readers firsthand adventure stories, top-notch wildlife photography, and in-depth articles about all things Alaska.

INDEX